Pearls of Wisdom

Collected by Harry Millner

Typeset in 12/14 pt Garamond by Letterpart Ltd., Reigate, Surrey.

Printed and bound in Great Britain by Cox & Wyman Ltd., Reading, Berkshire.

Clarion: published from behind no. 80 Brighton Road, Tadworth, Surrey, England. For information about our company and the other books we publish, visit our web site at www.clarion-books.co.uk

CONTENTS

PREAMBLE

What I offer here is a collection of wisdom which I have gathered from many sources over many years. They are pithy observations about life, and my intention is that they should be dipped into and savoured rather than ploughed through at lengthy readings.

This is a book for speech makers and essay writers who need pertinent truths to illustrate their points. It is also a book for anyone who wishes to reflect upon life's vagaries.

To make it manageable I have divided the sayings into subject groupings. Inevitably this has led to some repetition where a saying could equally well be included in many sections, but I have allowed myself to repeat any saying once or twice only, albeit occasionally in adjacent sections.

I hope you enjoy ambling through these thoughts on some of the greater things of life. As you go, remember: Life would be impossible without a sense of humour.

Ability

The archer is known by his ability – not his arrows.

Anyone can be a pilot in calm waters.

Many a person would be a rogue if he knew how.

The greatest scholars are not necessarily
the best preachers.

A dwarf on a giant's back sees further than both.

It takes more than gold braid to make a captain.

Give a man a fish and you feed him for a day. Give
him a fishing rod and you feed him for life.

Though a fool may try to act wise he is still a fool.

You can educate a person but you can't make
him think.

Acceptance

Acceptance is the death of ambition.

Acceptance is the secret of contentment.

How much easier to accept the misfortune of others.

Understanding is the beginning of acceptance.

One road to happiness is acceptance.

Oh well! No matter what happens there
is always death.

Napoleon

When I had money, they called me brother.

The wise man wants for nothing.

You are wise, if few things annoy you.

The question is not whether we have failed but whether
we are content with failure.

Pessimism, when you get used to it,
is just as good as optimism.

Arnold Bennett

We are all in the gutter – but some don't know it.

It is better to bend than to break.

The rich man's joke is always funny.

Habit is a great deadener.

Whoever is rich is my brother.

Greek saying

Given the choice, we usually follow the herd.

To know nothing is to doubt nothing.

What you can't avoid, welcome.

ACHIEVEMENT

All that a person leaves behind are his deeds.

There is pleasure in the pursuit of anything.

It's the last battle that counts.

One crowded hour of glorious life is worth an age without a name.

Well begun is half done.

Try to live every day of your life.

There are many paths to the top of the mountain – but only one view.

We can live like a lord, yet die like a fool.

The greatest talkers are often the least doers.

Start much and you will finish little.

For war, one side is enough; for peace, you need two.

It's not how you start, it's how you finish.

The reward for having done something well is having done it.

After the chase, the victory is often an anticlimax.

The harder the fight, the sweeter the victory.

Once something has been invented,
it cannot be disinvented.

We all love what we are good at.

ACTION

Don't give pity – give action.

Good deeds are better than good creeds.

The art of living is knowing how far to go – then going a little further.

The hinge that squeaks gets oiled first.

When skating on thin ice, speed is safety.

We can run, but not hide.

Don't give advice, give example.

What is not worth doing is not worth doing well.

The nail that sticks up gets hammered.

Our actions are never as good or as bad as our desires.

ADVANTAGE

A person surprised is half taken.

A man surrounded by pygmies looks big.

Many a person's misfortunes have kept him out of gaol.

Forewarned is forearmed.

If you have lent someone money and he avoids you,
you have been let off cheaply.

In the land of the blind, the one-eyed man is king.

Why travel when you're already there?

Better to be an old man's darling
than a young man's fool.

Mediocrity has its attractions – it's a lot less demanding than success.

Strength lies not in defence but in attack.

Adolf Hitler

ADVICE

A good fright is the best advice.

After it's done, it is too late for advice.

We can give the advice but not the wisdom to go with it.

Love can't take advice – and lovers won't.

Those who advise don't have to pay.

To ask advice is usually to seek flattery.

The conformer's head never aches.

A fool will always find someone more foolish to advise him.

Don't call an alligator a big-mouth until you have passed him.

Jamaican saying

Slowly, slowly catchee monkey.

Burmese saying

If silence is good for the wise, how much better for the fool!

If you can't swim, don't jump in the deep end.

The best cure for seasickness is find a tree and sit under it.

Jamaican saying

The old give advice because they can no longer give example.

Many receive advice but how many profit from it?

If you want people to think well of you, don't speak well of yourself.

Make someone laugh and you have a friend.

No man should make the same mistake once.

Groucho Marx

A used key does not rust.

Give a man enough rope and he will hang himself.

Don't slam the door – you might want to return.

Don't start a quarrel when the gun is loaded.

To pay in advance is to be served badly.

Treat your friends as if one day they might turn foe.

Humiliation is the biggest revenge.

One "No" saves a great deal of trouble.

In baiting the mousetrap, leave room for the mouse.

Ascend a step to choose a friend – descend a step to choose a wife.

Chinese saying

Never make a pretty woman your wife.

Jamaican saying

Keep your eyes open before marriage and closed after.

Hear much – say little.

If you escape from the lion's den, don't go back for your hat.

AMBITION

Security is the death of ambition.

Ambition is the last refuge of failure.

Oscar Wilde

Lack of ambition may be mistaken for patience.

The slave has one master – the ambitious has many.

To climb a ladder, we must start at the bottom.

To hit your target, aim a little above it.

The quality of a person is not in what he achieves but in what he wants to achieve.

Why kiss the maid when you can kiss the mistress?

Everyone is or hopes to be an idler.

Ambition is really hidden greed.

Habit is a great deadener.

If you stay in the valley, you won't get over the hill.

"My ambition," said Alice, "is to obtain the maximum comfort with the minimum exertion."

ANGER

Anger is an expensive luxury.

Anger punishes itself.

In anger, our true nature is revealed.

Anger usually ends in cruelty.

In anger, we lose reason.

Anger is not sudden but a build up of irritations.

Anger and temper will shorten life.

Don't try to pacify someone at the height of their anger.

If you are angry, the chances are you might be in the wrong.

Beware of the anger of a quiet person.

Laughter may signify anger.

By keeping your temper, you will increase theirs.

Anger nearly always ends in regret.

Anger is the enemy of persuasion.

Your anger is a weapon for your opponent.

Anticipation

Anticipation is the better part of pleasure.

Nothing is quite as good as it seemed beforehand.

It is the chase and not the catch that gives greatest pleasure.

Expectation is the better part of realisation.

An ounce of prevention is worth a pound of cure.

The lion and the lamb shall lie down together – but the lamb won't get much sleep.

Woody Allen

It is more tantalising to conceal than to reveal.

The reality is hardly ever as pleasant as the imaginary.

If Winter comes, can Spring be far behind?

Shelley

The anticipation of pain can be greater than the pain itself.

Appearance

A white beard doesn't make a person wise.

Only a millionaire can afford to look poor.

You are getting old when people start saying how well you look.

A wolf may lose his teeth but not his nature.

Good clothes will open many doors.

When things seem too good to be true
– they usually are.

Be a hypocrite – but don't look like one.

No-one is totally good or totally bad.

Secrets are betrayed by the face.

People see what we wear, not what we eat.

A thing is not worthwhile just because it is difficult.

Most charming people have something to conceal.

It must be great to be rich and not to have
to keep up appearances.

A person appears to you the way you appear to him.

You may not be one but you certainly look like one –
which is even worse.

Lord Queensberry to Oscar Wilde

A person is wise when he doesn't appear too clever.

Look wise and say nothing – speech is only useful
to conceal our thoughts.

A smile will make you look ten years younger.

One may appear sincere and still be stupid.

He has the kind of face – once seen
is never remembered.

Oscar Wilde

It's appearance, not truth, that counts.

Machiavelli

APPRECIATION

Appreciation makes for contentment.

To appreciate good fortune you must have known bad.

We often don't appreciate what we already have.

Dry bread at home is better than a feast abroad.

Home is not where we live but where we belong.

If you can't be grateful for what you have, be grateful for what you don't have.

Hunger is the best sauce.

What a wonderful life I've had
– if only I'd realised it sooner.

Judy Garland

I grumbled because I had no shoes – until I saw a man who had no feet.

Confucius

To enjoy the dawn you must have lived
through the night.

You will never persuade a mouse that a black cat is lucky.

We must experience the fear of death to appreciate being alive.

Never to have suffered is never to have been blessed.

Buddha

A likeable person is someone who likes you.

Weep for the man who doesn't know his good fortune.

Confucius

"You've got your eyesight and you are not in a wheelchair – so what's your problem?" asked Alice.

ARGUMENT

To resort to violence is to lose the argument.

An argument is an exchange of ignorance.

It is impossible to defeat an ignorant person in an argument.

If you have no basis for argument then turn to insults.

Ridicule is the first and last argument of a fool.

To get personal is to lose the argument.

A long dispute often means both parties are in the wrong.

Truth is lost when we argue.

There are always three sides to a story: yours, the other person's and the truth.

The test of a person's character is how he behaves in a quarrel.

Ridicule is more deadly than argument.

Don't quarrel with someone beneath you.

Quarrels are the weapons of the weak.

Quarrels would not last so long if the fault was only on one side.

ASSOCIATION

The nearer the king, the nearer the gallows.

Where the carcass is – that's where the vultures are gathered.

We become like those we associate with.

If you help a thief you are as bad as a thief.

A thief believes everybody else is a thief.

If you want to be thought wise, agree with them.

You need a long spoon to sup with the devil.

Don't deal with someone with nothing to lose.

You won't become a saint through others' sins.

A constant guest is never welcome.

We are known by the friends we keep.

There is a very fine line between genius and madness.
Aristotle

To deal with the tainted is to become tainted yourself.

Where there is honey, there are flies.

Every dog is a lion in his own home.

In the company of fools, a wise man looks foolish.

Mix with pigs and the muck will stick.

ATTITUDE

A smile will open many doors.

It is the little things that reveal our character.

Good manners are made up of petty sacrifices.

Bad manners spoil everything – even reason and justice.

Impertinence is often well meant.

There is something about success which is displeasing.

The upper classes have pleasure
– the lower classes have fun.

It's not what you give – it's the way you give it.

The only thing worse than a bad loser is a bad winner.

It's loss of interest – not age – that makes you age.

It is not the strongest who win but those who want it the most.

'Why waste time being sad?' said Alice.

I have simple tastes – I only like the best.

Barbara Cartland

You may be broke, but you don't have to be poor.

No-one can make you feel inferior without
your consent.

"I said to the man with only one shoe,
'You have lost a shoe.'
'No,' he said, 'I have found one.' "

Defence is always stronger than offence.

ATTRACTION

A woman's weakness is her strength.

Power is the ultimate aphrodisiac.

Kissinger

It's the bait that hides the hook.

The devil baits his hook with beauty.

People are seldom attracted to us by our doing favours.

The most beautiful bird gets caged first.

If we are too friendly we may attract
people we don't like.

There are many bores who are so obviously happy it's a pleasure to watch.

Jerome K Jerome

What first attracts us to people seldom
binds us to them.

It is hard to dislike someone who praises you.

Many things are sweetened by risk.

Everything that deceives may be said to enchant.

Plato

A man may resist a sound argument
yet fall at a single glance.

If you want to be popular, ask people questions.

First impressions last.

A person's weakness is often the most likeable thing about him.

There's a harlot in every woman
– that's their attraction.

Oscar Wilde

"What can I wear to make me look younger?" asked the Duchess.
"Wear a smile," said Alice

BEAUTY

Beauty comes from within.

Beauty is as beauty does.

Beauty is the promise of happiness.

Beauty is that which pleases.

Beauty opens locked doors.

Beauty provokes a thief more than money.

Beauty is best appreciated from a distance.

Beauty is best when silent.

Beauty and folly are generally companions.

With beauty must be the ability to take advantage of it.

A woman's beauty may be fatal to her.

Whatever you love is beautiful.

All heiresses are beautiful.

Health and wealth create beauty.

If Jack's in love, he is no judge of Jill's beauty.

The ability to see beauty is the ability to stay young.

One pig is beautiful to another pig.

Wealth infatuates as well as beauty.

We weep for the beauty that could be and the horrors that are.

Socrates

Beauty is better than luck.

It's so sad to see beauty wasted.

Beauty is the awareness of perfection.

Beauty must have a touch of innocence.

Beauty cannot be bought.

It's hard to be a pretty woman without causing a little trouble.

BEGGARS

The beggar does more for the giver than the giver for the beggar.

Every beggar is descended from some king – and every king from some beggar.

None but the beggar can really live at ease.

Be grateful for the beggar – he makes you feel superior.

Only beggars are really free.

If you are a beggar, you can't be bankrupt.

Sit a beggar at your table and he soon will put his feet on it.

It is annoying to give to a beggar
– and annoying not to.

What is got by begging costs dear.

Better to die a beggar than to live a beggar.

BEGINNING

Every journey starts with but a single step.

The hardest step is that over the threshold.

The beginnings of all things are small.

Every beginning ends something.

Well begun is half done.

All beginnings are difficult.

Love is sweet in the beginning but bitter at the ending.

A bad beginning makes a bad ending.

You can't hope to win unless you begin.

BEHAVIOUR

Perfect behaviour is born out of complete indifference.

Oscar Wilde

Too much courtesy is discourtesy.

When someone is very polite they are probably lying.

If you are often brave, this will be expected of you.

Prosperity often breeds bad manners.

When you lose, imitate the behaviour of the winner.

A slip of the tongue is never accidental.

No-one becomes bad all at once.

It is easy being virtuous when you have
no other choice.

There are times when to apologise is to be rude.

A crab can't be made to walk straight.

The winner is the person who knows how to quit.

It is not natural to be amiable to the same person
every day.

Morality is the herd instinct in the individual.

Nietzsche

Before you can love others, you must love yourself.

Those who shout the loudest usually
have the most to hide.

A lady is a woman who makes a man behave
like a gentleman.

We are yesterday's children.

If you want to be good, begin by assuming you are bad.

When you quarrel, always leave room for making up.

Admiration, like love, will soon wear out.

No-one can hurt you as much as you hurt yourself.

There is no such thing as a bad person – only a person acting badly.

We make more enemies by what we say than friends by what we do.

I prefer someone openly wicked than
a pretence of goodness.

George Bernard Shaw

There is never a single bully on his own – they come in groups – we still have the pack animal instinct.

It's poor taste to be clever all the time.

In crowds we revert to the primitive.

What can you expect from a pig but a grunt?

You cannot shake hands with a clenched fist.

Gandhi

One murder makes a villain – millions make a hero.

Joseph Stalin

All affectations are faults.

One may be too busy doing good to be good.

Be good and you'll be lonely.

It's a mistake trying to be more agreeable than you really are.

Belief

Belief is often a matter of taste.

Beliefs are harder to shake than knowledge.

We are what we believe we are.

It is fear or hopes which make belief.

Nothing is more firmly believed than
that which is least known.

We soon believe that which we desire.

I don't believe – but I have faith.

Graham Greene

To believe in goodness and decency
we must have innocence.

A belief is not true just because it is convenient.

Lack of belief is nothing new
but it is now more acceptable.

You may have no religion but still believe.

In wars over men's beliefs, women and children
are killed.

Those who believe in nothing still need someone to
believe in them.

Some things have to be believed to be seen.

The more we know, the less we believe.

The happy do not believe in miracles.

A person may be ready to die for an idea, provided he is not quite clear about it.

Truth often depends upon custom.

Superstition is part of being human.

Christianity might be a good thing if anybody tried it.

George Bernard Shaw

To begin with certainties you will end with doubt.

How sad to see a beautiful theory killed
by a brutal fact.

Aldous Huxley

If someone says you can make it, you don't have to believe them – but believe in yourself.

By trying to persuade others, we convince ourselves.

It takes great courage to believe in nothing.

When two sincere people argue over their beliefs, both are right.

A believable lie is better than a stupid fact.

Italian saying

To believe in God makes life much easier.

I'm an atheist in the day and a Catholic at night.

Brendan Behan

If you're going to be wrong, be wrong with confidence.

The greater the lie, the greater the chance
of it being believed.

Belief may be improved by doubt.

Religion is not about faith but about doubt.
Graham Greene

Religion is a good invention in times of stress.
George Bernard Shaw

✓ In fair weather it's easy to be an atheist.

The certainties of one age are the problems of the next.

BELONGING

Home is not where we live but where we belong.

Contentment often lodges more in cottages
than palaces.

Where you live determines who you are.

A warm welcome is the best meal.

The greatest poverty is being unwanted.

One pig is beautiful to another pig.

I'd never join any club who would have me
as a member.
Groucho Marx

The absent are always wrong.

BEWARE

Beware of the person who does not return your blow –
he will not forgive you or allow you to forgive yourself.

Bertrand Russell

Beware of the anger of a quiet person.

Hasty speech has been the downfall of many.

The higher up the tree, the thinner the branches.

If we are too friendly, we may attract people
we don't like.

Never do business with friends, relatives or neighbours.

If you ride a tiger, you can't dismount.

Chinese saying

Many kiss the hand they wish to cut off.

Give a thief a rope and he'll steal it.

He who knows how to flatter you will know
how to slander you.

He who laughs has not yet heard the bad news.

The lunatics are taking over the asylum.

The more you have, the more you have to lose.

Confucius says he who walks in the middle of the road
gets run over.

Beware of the person who speaks well of everyone.

Beware of the pious fool and the wise sinner.

BITTERNESS

Things are not always as bad as they seem – they are often worse.

The worst is not certain – but very likely.

Enjoy it while it lasts – because it never does.

Seeing someone succeed where we have failed – that's the real punishment.

The end of one misfortune is a step nearer the next.

It is the thought of what we have missed that makes our sadness.

Most things are bearable – except others' good fortune.

Life is a process of endless decay.

The two saddest words: "If only".

We are told to love our enemies and our neighbours – probably because they are the same people.

Who marries a widow and three children
marries four thieves.

Anything will fit a naked man.

Marriage has two days of happiness – the first day and the last.

We would be rich if we didn't have to eat.

Die young and leave a good looking corpse.

Those who advise don't have to pay.

Honeymoon for a month – trouble for life.

Don't blame the mirror for your looks.

We often begrudge others what we cannot enjoy ourselves.

When life appears to be treating you well – watch out!

In prosperity our friends know us – in adversity we know our friends.

Every luxury must be paid for
– and everything is a luxury.

Everything comes to the person who doesn't need it.

Revenge keeps your own wounds green.

The world is a sewer – and we're all dodging muck.

Nothing is quite as good as it seemed beforehand.

"How can you stop someone loving you?" asked the Duchess.
"Easy," said the Duke, "Marry them."

BLUFF

The object of oratory is not truth but persuasion.

Machiavelli

Barking dogs seldom bite.

A good denial is the best point in law.

To be able to succeed, it's important
that you appear successful.

Being thought witty allows us a greater opportunity to play the fool.

To be successful act big, think big, and talk big.

Aristotle Onassis

The wolf doesn't fear the dog but his bark.

If you can fake sincerity, you can fake anything.

Laurence Olivier

BORES

A bore is a person who talks when you want
him to listen.

A bore is a person who, when you ask him how he is, will tell you.

Every hero will become a bore eventually.

There is no bigger bore than a clever one.

We are all bores at different degrees.

There are many bores who are so obviously happy it's a pleasure to watch.

Jerome K Jerome

The most learned people are often the most boring.

Being bored is sometimes the price worth paying
for keeping out of trouble.

A person may lack the power of conversation but not the power of speech.

There is something rather boring about somebody else's happiness.

The thoughtless are rarely wordless.

George Bernard Shaw

BORROWING

The borrower is servant to the lender.

If you laugh when you borrow, you will cry when you repay.

Before you borrow from a friend, decide which you need most.

If you have a horse – you may borrow another.

Creditors have better memories than the borrowers.

Better to sleep without supper than rise in debt.

BRAVERY

The brave man perishes by the sword – the coward in his bed.

Some have been thought brave because they had not the courage to run away.

Curiosity will conquer fear even more than bravery will.

A hyena is brave before a dead lion.

If you are often brave, this will be expected of you.

A uniform provides half a man's valour.

It is better to face the danger once
than always live in fear.

In a just world there would be no need for bravery.

A hero is a fool who doesn't tell anyone
how afraid he is.

A hero is no braver than an ordinary person
– but is braver for just a little longer.

He's a hero because he is brave enough to be
a coward.

Joseph Heller's *Catch 22*

BUREAUCRACY

The more laws – the more offenders.

Bureaucracy is a giant mechanism run by pygmies.

Bad officials are elected by good citizens who don't
bother to vote.

It is the unhappy people who fear change most.

The best way to kill incentive is to take
it to a committee.

BUSINESS

Never do business with friends, neighbours or relatives.

No person on his death bed ever said,
'I should have paid more attention to business'.

Don't confuse bad management with fate.

The recipe for failure is trying to please everyone.

The higher up the ladder, the greater the fall.

Trusting a lot has ruined a lot.

The price of umbrellas goes up when it rains.

In selling a horse – praise its bad points.

Don't deal with someone with nothing to lose.

Business brings money but friendship hardly ever does.

Make friends of your clients but not
clients of your friends.

CAUTION

Be careful what you wish for – you might get it.

Love your neighbour – but choose
your neighbourhood.

If we say what we like, we may hear what we don't like.

Don't quarrel with someone beneath you.

Never let those under you do you a favour – it will cost you dearly.

The higher up the tree the monkey climbs, the more he shows his behind.

Hell is not as bad as the road that leads to it.

It is the bait that hides the hook.

Tell secrets and you become their servant.

You have not converted someone just because you have silenced him.

A small spark may burn down a forest.

We would do many a foolish thing
if it wasn't for principles.

Don't call an alligator a big-mouth until you have passed him.

Jamaican saying

If you can't swim, don't jump in the deep end.

Woe to the one no-one likes – but beware of the one everyone likes.

Better not to show your teeth if you can't fight.

The lion and the lamb shall lie down together
– but the lamb won't get much sleep.

Woody Allen

Don't ever slam the door – you might want to return.

Watch out for the fellow that lets you
do all the talking.

Don't test the depth of the water with both feet.

Talk too much and you will soon say something you didn't intend to.

Be careful when an enemy speaks kindly.

An ally has to be watched just as much as an enemy.

Love thy neighbour but don't get caught.

Give me six lines any man has written and I will hang him with them.

Cardinal Richelieu

The scars of others should teach us caution.

There is no rose without a thorn.

CHARACTER

It is the little things that reveal our character.

Many people have character and nothing else.

We reveal our character in our prejudices.

Our character is revealed by what we laugh at.

Few people have enough character to be idle.

A wolf may lose his teeth but not his nature.

No person becomes bad all at once.

The quality of a person is not in what he achieves but in what he wants to achieve.

Judge people by their questions rather than their answers.

Heredity is nothing but stored environment.

Put a label on a person and they usually live up to it.

An empty sack cannot stand straight.

In anger our true nature is revealed.

A crab cannot be made to walk straight.

The test of a person's character is how he behaves in a quarrel.

The reputation of being honest is more important than being honest.

Soberness conceals what drunkenness reveals.

It takes character to stand the rigours of indolence.

We often cope with adversity better than prosperity.

If you have no enemies, it probably means
you are a failure.

CHARITY

Charity is the very salt of riches.

Confucius

Charity is no cure for poverty.

Charity deals with the effect and not the cause.

Poverty was created to give the rich opportunity
for charity.

We have the ability to be charitable
without necessarily wanting to.

They give twice who give quickly.

Pity is the sweetest form of love.

To be like Christ is to be a Christian.

Money is neutral – it's what you do with it that counts.

Give a man a fish and you feed him for a day. Give
him a fishing rod and you feed him for life.

In charity there is no excess.

Francis Bacon

In all our doings, without charity we are nothing.

Bible

It is good to give – but not too much.

Charity to the deserving is not charity but justice.

CHARM

All charming people are spoiled – that's the secret of their charm.

Oscar Wilde

A smile will open many doors.

The art of pleasing is the art of deceiving.

By flattery you can get people to do good.

Beauty opens locked doors.

Scoundrels are always sociable.

The bigger the rogue, the more convincing he is.

If you want to be popular, pretend to be interested.

Make a person feel important and you have a friend.

Always be sincere – even if you don't mean it.

You don't have to be kind but you must appear to be.

Most charming people have something to hide.

Honey catches more flies than vinegar.

CHILDHOOD

Oh, for the innocence of our childhood! Sadly we get wiser every day.

Childhood is a kingdom where nobody dies.

Oh! To have the days of our childhood restored or be able to forget them.

Happiness is a right for children not a privilege.

Children at play are not playing
– their games are real.

It was always summer in our childhood.

Children love to learn but hate to be taught.

A child's world is much nicer than the real one.

There are no illegitimate children
– only illegitimate parents.

If a child tells a lie, don't call him a liar – tell him he has told a lie.

Children and fools have merry lives.

In extreme fear we revert to childhood.

Old age is but an extension of childhood.

They that have no children bring them up well.

Men never grow up – their toys just get bigger.

Innocence is a man's weakness but a child's strength.

Innocence is no protection.

My salad days – when I was green in judgment.

Shakespeare

Old men become children for the second time.

Childhood days, wild wood days among
the birds and bees.

Song

Sweet childish days, that were as long
As twenty days are now.

William Wordsworth

Those who dislike children dislike themselves.

How terribly sad – children without a childhood.

Oh, to retain the simplicity of a child!

Innocence is part of childhood.

The simplest questions may be the hardest to answer.

The secret of my success – I remained a child.

Albert Einstein

Only a child's life is a real life.

George Orwell

I had a wonderful childhood – except it had
nothing to do with being a child.

Liza Minnelli

Choice

Necessity leaves us no choice.

We only do what we want – given the choice.

We must choose between boredom or involvement.

Happiness is liking what you do and doing
what you like.

You can choose to begin love – but not to end it.

We don't live as we would like to but as we have to.

Christianity

Christianity might be a good thing if anybody tried it.
George Bernard Shaw

Christianity is a way of life much more than a religion.

The idea of Christ is much older than Christianity.

Jesus didn't start Christianity.

Christianity has done a great deal for love – by making
a sin out of it.

They suspect in others the faults they
could commit themselves.

I believe in Christ but not the Church.
George Bernard Shaw

Socialism is like Christianity – it has never been tried.
John Mortimer

Church

We must bypass the Church to find God.

The nearer the Church, the further from God.

The best Church is in our heart.

Many people go to church to air their finery.

If God is everywhere, why need a church?

An ale house won't harm a good person
– and a church won't benefit a bad one.

Churchgoers are no better than others
but suffer more guilt.

A lot of people are leaving the Church and going back to God.

Don't confuse piety with faith.

Company

Visitors always give pleasure – if not on
their arrival then on their departure.

You won't become a saint through others' sins.

In good company the journey is short.

Keep company with wolves and you'll learn to howl.

Solitude is sometimes the best company.

Without the company of fools a witty person may be lost.

Beauty and folly are generally companions.

He travels furthest who travels alone.

Coward, hold my coward's hand.

Loneliness makes strange bed fellows.

The trouble with being rich is having to mix with other rich.

Two fighting dogs become allies when a wolf comes along.

COMPARISONS

It is comparisons that make us happy or miserable.

A man surrounded by pygmies looks big.

There would be no great persons if there were no small persons.

I grumbled because I had no shoes – until I saw a man who had no feet.

Confucius

In the land of the blind the one-eyed man is king.

The smell of garlic keeps away the smell of onions.

To appreciate good fortune you must have known bad fortune.

The antidote for mental suffering is physical pain.

If you think you have problems wait till you hear the other person's.

CONCEIT

Conceit is the finest armour we can wear.

Conceit is the gift to the little man.

A conceited person is one of life's failures.

Too much modesty is conceit.

We only impress ourselves.

None are so empty as those who are full of themselves.

The most silent people are often those who think most highly of themselves.

Every donkey loves to hear himself bray.

When vices leave us, we flatter ourselves that we have left our vices.

We cherish our friends not for their ability to amuse us but for ours to amuse them.

When we praise someone we call ourself his equal.

A conceited person is someone who is more interested in himself than in me.

The poor think God is on their side
– the rich know he is.

Confession

By confessing small faults we give the impression we have no large ones.

Explaining is half confessing.

A fault confessed is half redressed.

It is the confession, not the priest, that gives absolution.

Confess to God and you will be forgiven.
Confess to man and you will be laughed at.

Who strikes first admits he is wrong.

Silence may be equal to confession.

Everyone has a need to confess.

Conscience

Conscience is the inner voice that warns us someone might be watching.

Conscience is its own punishment.

Conscience doesn't stop us doing what we should not – it just stops us from enjoying it.

Conscience and cowards are brothers.

Conscience is often the conforming with the opinions of others.

With a guilty conscience you live with fear.

People never do evil so readily as when they
do it in the name of conscience.

Blaise Pascal

A guilty person runs when no-one is chasing.

We would do many a silly thing if it wasn't
for principles.

A sin in private is not a sin.

Man is the only animal that blushes, or needs to.

Mark Twain

You will hate in a person that which is part
of yourself.

A thief is sorry that he is caught but not
that he is a thief.

Methought I heard a voice cry 'Sleep no more;
Macbeth does murder sleep'.

Shakespeare

CONSEQUENCE

Punishment always follows excess.

Sing in the summer and you will cry in the winter.

To chain someone down you must wear
the same chain.

Pardon the offence and you will encourage more.

Every light has its shadow.

Sit a beggar at your table and he'll soon
put his feet on it.

Save a thief from the gallows and he will live to cut
your throat.

It is hard to be efficient without being unpopular.

Shame follows pride.

The price we pay may ruin our pleasure.

None are safe from flatterers.

If you deceive others, you also deceive yourself.

Man who pats himself on back risks broken arm.

Chinese saying

Who lives alone is either a saint or a devil.

Keep company with wolves and you'll learn to howl.

It's all that sunshine that makes the desert.

Laugh now – cry later.

If you dig a pit, you might fall into it.

Bible

Who lends loses double.

Those who dislike children dislike themselves.

For every victim there is more than one victim.

Fear is the parent of cruelty.

Confucius says he who walks down the middle of the road gets run over.

People who think themselves terribly important are the first to have breakdowns.

There's no escaping – the devil always pays his dues.

Repentance is not so much remorse as fear of the consequences.

Today's fire will be tomorrow's ashes.

Revenge is its own executioner.

CONSOLATION

Looking unhappy is sometimes a consolation for being unhappy.

Bad habits in others are often a consolation to us.

The thought of suicide is a great consolation.

The poor man's envy may be eased by the hope of the rich man's downfall.

The poor will have the best seats in paradise.

The suffering of the rich is among the sweetest pleasures of the poor.

On our last journey we won't need to pack anything.

You may lose everything but find yourself.

Broken bones become stronger.

Even when you lose there may be some gain.

I cried all the way to the bank.

Liberace

The sharper the storm, the sooner it is over.

Barking dogs seldom bite.

If you have no money, you won't need a purse.

You won't skid, if you stay in a rut.

There are more old drunkards than old doctors.

You can't go through a difficult time without getting something out of it.

The one-legged never stumble.

We are not satisfied with being right, unless we can prove that the other is wrong.

"I'm sure the grapes are sour," said the fox.

Aesop

The first shall be last and the last shall be first.

Bible

CONTENTMENT

Contentment often lodges more in cottages than palaces.

To be poor and content is to be rich indeed.

Buddha

Appreciation makes for contentment.

A contented life would be a life of busy solitude.

Contentment is the nearest we can get to paradise in this world.

To chase after happiness is to run from contentment.

Acceptance is one secret of contentment.

If you are foolish enough to be contented,
don't show it but grumble with the rest.

It takes contentment to be idle.

Enough is as good as a feast.

Ignorance is the peace of life.

Success is being able to spend your time your own way.

Contentment is liking what you do.

The greatest wealth is the contentment with little.

If you're contented with little, you have enough.

A Jug of Wine, a Loaf of Bread – and Thou
Beside me singing in the Wilderness –
Oh, Wilderness were Paradise enow!

***Edward Fitzgerald** – Omar Khayyám*

"A chicken curry, some cans of beer – that's the nearest I'll get to paradise!" said Albert.

To want for nothing is to have everything.

Buddha

Cost

Nothing costs more than that which we are given.

Even a bargain costs money.

What is got by begging costs dear.

A good word costs no more than a bad one.

What is cheap may be too expensive.

Many a priceless thing may be bought.

Every luxury must be paid for
– and everything is a luxury.

Good bargains empty purses.

What price can we pay for our soul?

Bible

If you want to dance you must pay for the music.

Tears will not repay debts.

The price we pay for money is our freedom.

We can't afford to have things given us.

Illness may be the price we pay for pleasure.

There is no such thing as a free lunch.

Milton Friedman

Free love may be love but it's never free.

Quality is remembered long after the price is forgotten.

You always pay for your stupidity one way or another.

If you can afford it, it's not worth buying.

Duchess of Windsor

For every loss there is some gain and for every gain there is some loss.

Free offers always come with a price tag.

If you pay peanuts, you get monkeys.

Everything is free – until you come to pay for it.

COURAGE

Courage is halfway between cowardice and stupidity.

Courage and skill are worth little without luck.

He who has never been in danger cannot answer for his courage.

Despair will give a coward courage.

The test of courage is not how you die but how you live.

One person with courage makes a majority.

The strongest person is he who stands alone.

We often cope with adversity better than prosperity.

He travels furthest who travels alone.

The hardest step is that over the threshold.

Without power, try to act brave.

It is better to die in honour than to live in shame.

If someone says you can make it, you don't have to believe them – but believe in yourself.

It's not the distance but the first step that matters.

You may be down but not out.

To be in the minority probably means you are in the right.

It takes great courage to believe in nothing.

If you fall down, don't stay down.

If more people had had courage, Hitler would have remained a corporal.

Courage is not the absence of fear but the ability to carry on with dignity in spite of it.

Better to die on your feet than to live on your knees.

COWARDS

Cowards die many times before their deaths.

Shakespeare

Cowardice is the best protection against temptation.

A coward is a person who thinks with his legs.

All bullies are cowards.

Many would be a coward, if they had the courage to run away.

Pacifism is simply a disguise for cowardice.

Adolf Hitler

Coward hold my coward's hand.

Each man kills the thing he loves . . . the coward does it with a kiss.

Oscar Wilde

The brave man perishes by the sword – the coward in his bed.

Tolerance is often a form of cowardice.

Despair will give a coward courage.

To be truly brave one must be part coward.

Conscience and cowards are brothers.

Opportunity and necessity make cowards brave.

Hatred is the coward's revenge for being frightened.

War is a coward's way of escaping the problems of peace.

Give a man a mask and he will speak the truth.

When the lights are out, the mice will dance.

You can't be a hero without being a coward.

A hyena is brave before a dead lion.

When in trouble, the wicked repent.

When we are afraid we say we are cautious
– when others are, we say they are cowards.

A coward may not be glorious
but he will remain healthy.

CRIME

A crime is something someone else commits.

Successful crimes alone are justified.

Why take up crime when there are legal
ways of being dishonest?

Commit an offence twice and it won't seem a crime.

There are no great criminals – only great crimes.

The greatest crimes are often caused by having too
much rather than having too little.

If poverty is the main cause of crime, stupidity is the
next.

You may commit a criminal offence
without being a criminal.

Public robbery is called financial skill.

The receiver is as bad as the thief.

Guns don't kill people – people kill people.

Those who steal to live do not necessarily sin.

St Aquinas

You may do an evil thing without being evil.

What crimes are committed in the name of liberty!

Praiseworthy deeds in war are punishable
crimes in peace.

To accept an evil is as bad as doing that evil.

Behind every great fortune is a great crime.

Without a victim, how can there be a crime?

Rape is a crime against the mind, not the body.

CROWDS

In crowds we lose our mind and get another one.

In crowds we revert to primitive.

There is cruelty in crowds – though each individual
may not be so.

Where there is a crowd there is untruth.

Individual people in crowds become evil.

It is not necessary for a crowd to know what they are
cheering about.

We all have mob self and individual self in us.

Tyranny leads by following the mob.

Cunning

More fights are won by giving in.

If you want the daughter, flatter the mother.

The weak who know how to play on their weakness become strong.

Keep quiet and you will be thought a thinker.

Be a hypocrite but don't speak like one.

Pretend to believe a liar – he will then lie even more and reveal himself.

In selling a horse – praise its bad points.

We often praise others in the hope
of praising ourselves.

If you are foolish enough to be content,
don't show it but grumble with the rest.

The devil has the best tunes.

General Booth

Flattery is a device for theft.

The wisest prophets make sure of the event beforehand.

Have an open face but conceal your thoughts.

Never interrupt an enemy when he is making a mistake.

To refuse praise is to desire to be praised even more.

If you don't say anything, you won't be asked to repeat it.

The secret of being considered efficient is to make the job look harder than it is.

A clever liar doesn't go into details.

To hit a bullseye – fire the arrow first, then draw the target round it.

It takes a clever person to lie well.

Don't be too clever for your own good.

The devil hides behind the cross.

The height of cleverness is to be able to conceal it.

You can get rich from work – often from someone else's.

If you want to get people behind you – invent a common enemy.

CYNICISM

Cynics are only contented when making the world as barren for others as they have for themselves.

Cynicism is often an unpleasant way of seeing the truth.

Cynicism is disappointed idealism.

Turn a cynic inside out and he becomes a sentimentalist.

Most things are funny, if they happen to someone else.

Consultation is often getting approval for what has already been decided.

When your neighbour's house is on fire, try not to show too much pleasure.

They that have no children bring them up well.

All work and no play makes Jack a dull boy – and Jill a wealthy widow.

Poor relatives are distant relatives.

A lot of troubles are man-maid.

Why buy a cow when milk is so cheap?

Few things matter very much – and most things not at all.

A good deed seldom goes unpunished.

Diplomacy is the art of getting someone else to think like you.

Why take up crime when there are legal ways of being dishonest?

There are more votes in making people laugh than making them think.

All heiresses are beautiful.

A rich widow cries with one eye and laughs with the other.

It would be advisable if you showed more affection than you felt.

Logic is the art of going wrong with confidence.

Tolerance is the virtue of the person with no convictions.

If you really must do wrong, then at least try to enjoy it.

Being grateful is often a wish to get more benefits.

When the legend conflicts with the facts, stick to the legend.

What is cheap may be too expensive.

Women inspire men to greatness – then prevent them from achieving it.

The conformer's head never aches.

The smell of garlic keeps away the smell of onions.

All women are the same height lying down.

Most kindness is doubtful.

If you lie on the ground, you can fall no lower.

Who is rich is not called a fool.

While a cow can be milked, it won't be slaughtered.

Success is the best revenge.

Idealism increases the further from the problem.

We spend the first half of our lives collecting things – and the second half trying to get rid of them.

Small minds are troubled by small things.

A man doesn't comfort a pretty widow
just out of kindness.

The lunatics are taking over the asylum.

Marriage is the only adventure open to the coward.

Voltaire

"I always believe the worst because the worst is usually true," said Alice.

The reason I drink is because I will soon be dead and then won't be able to drink any more.

Dylan Thomas

If it's too good to be true – it usually is.

Being nice to people is often another way of lying.

I have a beautiful wife – everybody loves her.

'I feel like a million dollars,' he said, 'in used notes!'

Three can keep a secret – if two are dead.

Hells Angels' motto

If someone is no good at their job
– make them management.

The best soldiers must have no imagination.

Soldier's opinion

Happiness always comes too late.

When I start feeling happy I ask myself,
"Where's the catch?"

To the jaundiced, all things are yellow.

Never let the facts get in the way of a good story.

Danger

Danger makes people devout.

The half fool and half wise are dangerous.

In times of danger, enemies become friends.

He thinks too much: such men are dangerous.
Shakespeare

When someone has nothing to lose,
he is doubly dangerous.

We are never more in danger than when we feel secure.

The lone sheep is in danger from the wolf.

The love of the wicked is more dangerous
than their hate.

Everyone represents a danger to someone.

A good servant makes a dangerous enemy.

He who has never been in danger cannot
answer for his courage.

Too much happiness is dangerous.

It is better to face the danger once,
than always live in fear.

The higher up the tree – the thinner the branches.

Don't start a quarrel when the gun is loaded.

In moments of crisis, fear is blocked out.

The devil's boots don't creak.

We never know what is enough, until we have had more than enough.

Old men are dangerous because they no longer care what happens to the world.

Nowadays it may be safer to be a soldier on the battlefield than a civilian in the market place.

Nothing is more dangerous than an idea when it's the only one.

DEATH

The greatest loss in life is not death but what dies inside us while we live.

Death is God's last gift to the living.

Death usually comes too early or too late.

Death must be distinguished from dying.

Death is nature's way of telling us to slow down.

Death pays all debts.

Death is the great leveller.

Death is an extension of life.

To live in someone's heart is not to die.

Oh well! No matter what happens
there is always death.

Napoleon

We begin to die, once we give up our desires.

Once we accept our death, we become free to live.

Money is something you need in case you
don't die tomorrow.

They should weep at our birth and not at our death.

Repent before you die – maybe today.

Every great artist has been helped by being dead.

If you don't think about death,
you won't appreciate life.

If you live long enough, sooner or later you will die of
too much living.

Try to die young at a very old age.

No person on his death bed ever said, ' I should have
paid more attention to business.'

Nothing dies.

Die young and leave a good looking corpse.

We differ from all other creatures because we know we
are mortal.

On your last journey you don't need to pack anything.

Sweet is the sleep that knows no pain.

In my end is my beginning.

Mary Queen of Scots

Immortality is what we leave behind.

He that believeth in me shall not die but have everlasting life.

Jesus

The best is yet to come.

All men are equal in the presence of death.

Drink! For once dead you never shall return.

Edward Fitzgerald – *Omar Khayyám*

It is not how a man dies but how he lives that matters.

In the midst of life we are in death.

Bible

Consider this your last day and you'll be ready to forgive.

Time doesn't go. Time stays – we go.

Every time we say goodbye I die a little.

Song

Truth sits upon the lips of dying men.

It is boredom, not hard work, that kills.

The first breath is the beginning of death.

The last enemy that is destroyed is death.

Bible

Our loved ones don't die – they look on and help us.

To die is to be promoted to glory.

Salvation Army

A useless life is an early death.

Six feet of earth makes all men equal.

Memento mori – remember we all must die.

The longer you live, the sooner you'll die.

Who is not forgotten is not dead.

We all think we are immortal – until we reach forty.

It's not only the dead who die.

We must experience the fear of death to appreciate being alive.

Those whom the gods love die young.

DEBTS

Debts will shorten your life.

Tears will not repay your debts.

Death pays all debts.

You are rich if you have no debts.

The worst form of poverty is to be in debt.

DECEIT

The art of pleasing is the art of deceiving.

We are not deceived by others but by ourselves.

Those who flatter you more than usual have either deceived you or wish to.

Life is the art of being deceived.

Many kiss the hand they wish to cut off.

Perhaps we all prefer being deceived.

Sweetness is often a disguise for weakness.

Some people can't tell the truth without lying.

Always speak your mind – even if you don't mean it.

Pride often wears the cloak of humility.

Flatterers look like friends, in the same way as wolves look like dogs.

To speak ill of someone is a dishonest way of praising ourselves.

I much prefer a lying compliment to a sincere criticism.
Oscar Wilde

You can tell if someone makes a mistake but not if they are lying.

Nothing is easier than self-deception.

Everything that deceives may be said to enchant.
Plato

The worst adultery is making love while thinking of another.

An insincere kiss is worse than an honest blow.

A woman's tears are a form of bribery.

It is easier to believe strangers because they have not yet deceived us.

DECISIONS

A man is as big as his decisions.

Churchill

Our destiny sometimes depends upon the most trivial of decisions.

Most human acts involve more chance than decision.

What may be done at any time may never be done.

Every journey starts with but a single step.

When you have made up your mind, don't confuse yourself with facts.

Pencil me in a definite maybe.

Samuel Goldwyn

We must choose between boredom or involvement.

A conclusion is when you get tired of thinking.

Say no the first time and you won't get troubled again.

It is not the distance but the first step that matters.

If you stay in the valley, you won't get over the hill.

Worry is fear without a decision.

DEEDS

All that a person leaves behind are his deeds.

Good deeds are better than good creeds.

We may not be responsible for our thoughts but we are for our deeds.

Good deeds remain good deeds,
no matter what the motive.

A good deed seldom goes unpunished.

What you do to others, you do to yourself.

To think evil is much the same as doing it.

If we make no mistakes, we make nothing.

An injury to one is an injury to all.

Am I my brother's keeper?

Cain

The first blow is half the battle.

Most things are easy if done willingly.

We do more things through habit
than we do through reason.

Rob me of the price but not of the quality.

The hinge that squeaks the most gets mended first.

It takes more than gold braid to make a captain.

A hero is no braver than an ordinary person
but braver for just a little longer.

Energy creates energy.

No-one wins who doesn't fight.

The way we give is more important than the gift itself.

Try to live as if this was your last day.

It is not what a man does but what he would do which exalts him.

No-one is useless who lightens the burden of another.

What can you expect from a pig but a grunt?

Better to live one day as a lion than a hundred years as a sheep.

An insincere kiss is worse than an honest blow.

Handsome is as handsome does.

How much harm may be done by doing good!

In all our doings, without charity we are nothing.

Bible

Don't make two sorrows out of one.

One crowded hour of glorious life is worth an age without a name.

Wise men walk while fools sleep.

The only thing necessary for the triumph of evil is for the good to do nothing.

It's not your looks but your deeds
that make you human.

You may commit a criminal offence
without being a criminal.

Doing good is also a form of vanity.

Everything we do is done with an eye
to something else.

The only person who doesn't make a mistake is the person who does nothing.

We are disliked as much for the good we do as for the harm we do.

DEFENCE

Laughter may be a defence mechanism.

Strength lies not in defence but in attack.

Adolf Hitler

We prefer strangers because they have not yet hurt us.

Drink helps us to like ourselves a little more – for just a little while more.

Don't defend yourself before you have been accused.

To deny your guilt is to double it.

To excuse yourself is to accuse yourself.

We often make jokes about the things that frighten us.

Religion is a good invention in times of stress.

We need scapegoats to purge ourselves
of our own guilt.

DESIRES

The unobtainable is always the most desirable.

Our actions are never as good or as bad as our desires.

Strong hates reveal our secret desires.

Discontent arises more from our desires
than from our needs.

Some desires are necessary to make life worth living.

He is rich who desires little.

Buddha

Riches increase rather than satisfy our desires.

We begin to die, once we give up our desires.

Happiness is being able to admire without desiring.

Hope is as cheap as desire.

Desire is another form of fear.

It is the forbidden that is most desirable.

What we desire but cannot have
– that we then ridicule.

To want for nothing is to have everything.

Buddha

The more we have, the more we want.

Wanting soon becomes a habit.

Contentment is to want for nothing.

Greed grows by what it feeds on.

Having the least desires takes us nearer to paradise.

To be without some of the things you want is an indispensable part of happiness.

Bertrand Russell

Forbid something and it becomes desirable.

Much of desire is visual.

Isn't it sad that desire should long outlive performance?

"Protect me from my wants," said Alice.

As long as I have a want I have reason for living.
Satisfaction is death.

George Bernard Shaw

If you want something badly enough, you will get it.

The things we desire are often more dangerous than the things we fear.

Desperation

We are all living a life of quiet desperation.

George Bernard Shaw

Hope is the last gift given to man.

Extreme hopes are born from extreme miseries.

The thought of suicide is a great consolation.

We laugh sometimes that we may not weep.

Don't push a lapdog too far
– he may turn into a Rottweiler.

Men rattle their chains to show they are free.

To resort to violence is to lose the argument.

If you think you are going mad, you must be sane.

***Joseph Heller's** Catch 22*

Aggression is the last resort of the ignorant.

The miserable have no other medicine
But only hope.

Shakespeare

He who only hopes is hopeless.

"He must have been very desperate to do that," said the Duchess.
"Most people are," said Alice.

"Freedom" is just another word for
"nothing left to lose".

DEVIL

We never hear the devil's side of the story.

If you play with the devil, you'll end up in hell.

Jamaican saying

The devil dances on an empty purse.

The devil hides behind the cross.

The devil's boots don't creak.

The devil sometimes speaks the truth.

The devil tempts us so he may punish us.

You will always find money for the devil.

The devil has the best tunes.

General Booth

The devil tempts all, but an idle person tempts the devil.

The Lord sends the food and the devil sends the cook.

The devil can quote scriptures for his purpose.

The devil looks after his own.

The devil baits his hook with beauty.

You will need a long spoon if you sup with the devil.

When you gamble you share with the devil.

It is better to flatter the devil than to fight him.

The devil is an optimist if he thinks he can
make people meaner than they are.

The devil's greatest victory is to persuade
us he doesn't exist.

Only the devil has luck – God doesn't need it.

DIPLOMACY

Diplomacy is the art of getting someone
else to think like you.

Knowing how to refuse is as important as knowing how
to accept.

Discussions are a way of making others see that they
are wrong.

If you want to be thought wise, agree with them.

More fights are won by giving in.

A soft answer turneth away wrath.

Bible

The best way to entertain some people
is to listen to them.

It would be advisable if you showed more affection
than you felt.

A good word costs no more than a bad one.

When you quarrel, always leave room for making up.

Knowing how to refuse a favour is a very useful art.

Never claim as a right what you can get as a favour.

Good manners consist in concealing how much we think of ourselves and how little we think of others.

Mark Twain

It takes a clever woman to handle a foolish man.

The wise know what to overlook.

If you want people to think well of you, don't speak well of yourself.

If you want to get people behind you – invent a common enemy.

Anger is the enemy of persuasion.

DISTANCE

Distance lends enchantment.

Distance helps to keep our friends near.

We often agree with each other better from a distance.

Onlookers see more than the players.

Beauty is best appreciated from a distance.

The longest way often ends up as the shortest.

Respect is greater from a distance.

Idealism increases the further the problem.

Don't look too far ahead – take one step at a time.

Dogma

Dogma is not a religion but a religious disease.

Oscar Wilde

Nothing is more dangerous than an idea
when it's the only one.

We have boxes in our minds with labels on them.

Fanaticism is the extreme form of censorship.

Truth turns into dogma as soon as it is disputed.

Nationalism is the disease of mankind.

When we say 'to die for our country' we really mean
'to kill for our country'.

The doctrine of an eye for an eye
leaves everybody blind.

Martin Luther King

We use the word 'principle' when we
cannot use reason.

Doubt

Doubt is the key to knowledge.

Through doubt we may learn.

A philosopher is one who doubts.

A doubter might come closer
to God than all the churchgoers.

Knowledge grows with doubt.

Pencil me in a definite maybe.

Samuel Goldwyn

To begin with certainties, you will end with doubt.

I am an unbeliever but sometimes I have doubts.

George Bernard Shaw

The trouble is the fools are sure
and the learned have doubts.

People become fanatics when they have doubts.

Belief may be improved by doubt.

Religion is not about faith but about doubt.

Graham Greene

Doubt everything.

Descartes

DREAMS

Dreams lift up fools.

Dreams help us renew our sanity.

To dream is happiness – to wake is reality.

We are such stuff as dreams are made on.

Shakespeare

Man is a make-believe animal
– his dreams are his hopes.

Without dreams, how unbearable life would be.

Happy are those who live in their world of dreams.

We are never old in our dreams.

Dreaming carries us pleasantly through life.

I'll see you in my dreams.

Song

You can't fill your purse with dreams.

Dreams are necessary for our survival.

A man is no better than his dreams.

DRINK

Drink helps us like ourselves a little bit more – for just a little while more.

Drink makes a person better pleased with himself – if not better pleased with others.

Drink is a possible way of destroying our life and other people's.

One drink is enough, two drinks are too many, and three drinks are not enough.

Portuguese saying

In drink, we mistake words for truth.

Drink and money make wise men fools.

Drink! For once dead you never shall return.

Edward Fitzgerald – *Omar Khayyám*

I drink to make people bearable.

Richard Burton

If only I could get a hangover,
I wouldn't drink so much.

Richard Burton

A drink makes the old young.

When drink goes in, secrets come out.

In drink there is a brief interlude
in believing in dreams.

A drunkard's purse is in the bottle.

The road to hell is paved with empty wine bottles.

Some people abuse alcohol and alcohol
abuses some people.

There are more old drunkards than old doctors.

A teetotaller rarely possesses great wisdom.

Better to die of good wine than a bad illness.

A drunk person will say what a sober
person is thinking.

A drunk will be sober next day – but a fool
will remain a fool.

Ah, my beloved! Fill the cup that clears today
of past regrets and future fears.

Edward Fitzgerald – *Omar Khayyám*

Soberness conceals what drunkenness reveals.

The reason I drink is because I will soon be dead and then won't be able to drink any more.

Dylan Thomas

When you drink not to feel good but just to feel normal – that's the problem.

"I never drink before 6pm," said the Duke. "Thank goodness it's 6pm somewhere!"

I feel sorry for people who don't drink – because when they get up in the morning that's the best they will feel all day.

Frank Sinatra

Water is all right in moderation.

Mark Twain

If you have good health and the price of a drink, death and love can be mourned in comfort.

Brendan Behan

Enemies

Few can do us good – but many can do us harm.

We make more enemies by what we say than friends by what we do.

Small gifts will make friends – a large one will make an enemy.

There are no small enemies.

Everyone represents a danger to someone.

A good servant makes a dangerous enemy.

Keep your friends close – and your enemies closer.

Sicilian saying

By lending, you could make an enemy.

In times of danger, enemies become friends.

If you have no enemies, it probably means you are a failure.

Our enemy's opinion of us may be the truth.

The strongest bond of friendship is having a mutual enemy.

A person's wealth is his enemy.

We are our own executioner.

It is better to make a weak man your enemy
than your friend.

It is better to have a hundred enemies outside the house than one inside.

We are our own worst enemy – we dig our own grave.

Better to have a good enemy than a bad friend.

Be careful when an enemy speaks kindly.

If you have no money to lend, you won't make an enemy.

Never interrupt an enemy when
he is making a mistake.

An ally has to be watched just as much as an enemy.

Let your enemy in, so you can keep him out.

Russian saying

My enemy's enemies are my friends.

All creatures have their natural enemies
– man is everyone's.

ENJOYMENT

The fullest enjoyment is obtained
by reducing your ego.

There is no cure for birth or death
but to enjoy the interval.

All animals except man know the purpose of life is to enjoy it.

Don't put off until tomorrow what can be enjoyed today.

One can bear sorrow – but it takes two to be glad.

If you enjoy work, it is not work.

Enjoyment is enriched by imagination.

No person is a failure who enjoys life.

What discomfort we put up with in order to say we have enjoyed ourselves!

Laughter is the cheapest luxury we can enjoy.

Money is the sixth sense which helps us enjoy the other five.

Wealth is not what you have but what you enjoy.

Conscience does not stop us doing what we should not do – it just stops us from enjoying it.

Forbidden fruits taste sweetest.

Most of us enjoy the inferiority of our friends.

How many people's lives have been brightened by other people's indiscretions!

We are here for a short time – let's get all the laughter we can.

If you want to dance, you must pay for the music.

If you really must do wrong,
then at least try to enjoy it.

An immoral person is someone who
is enjoying himself.

Enjoy it while it lasts
– because it never does.

We often begrudge others that which
we can't enjoy ourselves.

It is impossible to enjoy idling thoroughly unless one has plenty of work to do.

Jerome K Jerome

The upper classes have pleasures – the lower classes have fun.

Most things are funny if they happen to someone else.

The joy of possession seldom lasts.

If you enjoy it, it must be sinful.

ENVY

Happiness vanishes when envy appears.

They that envy are always poor.

By enjoying envy we admit we are inferior.

Don't envy the sinner – who knows what awaits him.

The poor man's envy may be eased by the hope of the rich man's downfall.

Most things are bearable – except others' good fortune.

Prosperity makes few friends.

We may be less upset by our own poverty than by the wealth of others.

Miserable people hate the cheerful.

It is comparisons that make us happy or miserable.

Nothing is more annoying than someone with less intelligence but with more sense than us.

Better to be envied than to be pitied.

"I'm sure the grapes are sour," said the fox.

Aesop

Envy is passive greed.

Your neighbour's apples always look the sweetest.

EQUALITY

Six foot of earth makes us all equal.

If we were all naked, how could we tell who were the kings?

We are all Adam's children.

The maid is as good as the mistress in the dark.

We hate those who make us feel inferior.

I am free from prejudice – I dislike everyone equally.

W C Fields

Once made equal to men, women become
their superiors.

Socrates

In heaven an angel is nobody in particular.

All men are equal in the presence of death.

We are all descended from apes.

Inferiors revolt that they may be equal and equals revolt
that they may be better.

Voltaire

ESCAPE

In drink there is a brief interlude in believing
in dreams.

You can run but not hide.

Work is a refuge for people with nothing better to do.

Oscar Wilde

Ah, my beloved! Fill the cup that clears today
of past regret and future fears.

Edward Fitzgerald – *Omar Khayyám*

EXCUSES

To excuse yourself is to accuse yourself.

Bad excuses are worse than none.

Tomorrow is the busiest day of the year.

Spanish saying

A bad carpenter never has a good saw.

We dislike many things in order not
to dislike ourselves.

Don't blame the mirror for your looks.

The guilty make excuses before they are accused.

When we do something we are ashamed of,
we often call it our duty.

Every act has an explanation for it.

What may be mistaken for shyness
may be plain selfishness.

When we get frightened we look for scapegoats.

Love blinds us to reason.

To show resentment is to admit you deserve it.

Never explain and never apologise.

Queen Victoria

We may excuse an inhuman act
by saying we are merely human after all.

EXPERIENCE

Experience is the name we give our mistakes.

Experience is a great teacher
but the price may be too high.

Experience helps us recognise
our mistakes when we do them again.

We are all prisoners of our experience.

Without experience there is little wisdom.

Next to knowing when to seize an opportunity, the
most important thing is knowing when to forgo
an advantage.

Today is the scholar of yesterday.

A cripple in the right direction
beats a runner in the wrong one.

An old poacher makes the best game keeper.

If you don't learn from the past, you will repeat it.

No person is born wise.

Old friends are best friends.

Lessons are not given, they are learnt.

What costs nowt is worth nowt.

Those who complain about women
usually have a particular one in mind.

The most fascinating women
seldom make the best wives.

The best way to profit is through others' folly.

A stumble may prevent a fall.

Cheerful people can be just as annoying
as miserable ones.

You can't go through a difficult time without getting
something out of it.

FAILURE

Failure is not the only punishment – there is also the success of others.

Through failure we may possibly succeed.

The question is not whether we have failed but whether we are content with our failure.

No person is a failure who enjoys life.

You can learn more from failure
than you can from success.

The tragedy is not in failing completely
but in only just missing.

If you have no enemies, it probably
means you are a failure.

Failures are usually the most conceited people.

Fear of failure leads to failure.

No person is a failure who is loved.

It is our failures that make us human.

Failing doesn't make you a failure.

The recipe for failure is trying to please everybody.

Success which costs too much must
be considered failure.

Ambition is the last refuge of failure.

Oscar Wilde

You must know failure, before you know success.

Think small and you stay small.

You may lose everything but find yourself.

If you lie on the ground, you can fall no lower.

Failure teaches us that we will all probably fail again.

Perhaps we may only learn through failure.

If someone is a gracious loser, he is probably a failure.

FAITH

Faith is belief without evidence.

Faith in a cause may be a substitute
for belief in ourselves.

Faith is not the same as goodness.

I don't believe – but I have faith.

Graham Greene

Don't confuse piety with faith.

We may change our faith, without changing our God.

Martyrs create faith, more than faith creates martyrs.

Crosses are ladders that reach to heaven.

Vision is the art of seeing the invisible.

Pope Pius X

The heart sees better than the eyes.

Prayer is in your heart – not on your knees.

Prayer is better than sleep.

Confucius

I am an unbeliever – but sometimes I have doubts.

George Bernard Shaw

To love well is to pray well.

Reason is the greatest enemy of faith.

All religions lead to God.

Once people begin to reason, all is lost.

Voltaire

I haven't got a religion – I have a faith.

Bertrand Russell

I'm an atheist in the day and a Catholic at night.

Brendan Behan

FAMILIARITY

Familiarity in a superior is resented – because it cannot be returned.

In heaven an angel is nobody in particular.

Most things are clever only for the first time.

The priest's friend loses his faith.

Mix with pigs and the muck will stick.

A constant guest is never welcome.

Admiration, like love, will soon wear out.

Every hero will become a bore eventually.

Nothing is wonderful once you get used to it.

Repeat a thing often enough and it becomes the truth.

FANATICISM

Fanaticism consists in doubling your effort when you have forgotten your aim.

Fanaticism is the extreme form of censorship.

From fanaticism to barbarism is but a single step.

The worst vice of a fanatic is his sincerity.

Zeal is fit for the wise but found mainly in fools.

We are often intolerant in support of tolerance.

A person may be ready to die for an idea – provided he is not quite clear about it.

Terrorism is a product of democracy.

People become fanatics when they have doubts.

FATE

Fate deals the cards.

When fate picks your name out of the hat – that's it!

Most human acts involve more chance than decision.

Our destiny sometimes depends upon the most trivial of decisions.

Don't confuse bad management with fate.

There's a risk in crossing the street and there's a risk in not crossing the street.

The anticipated seldom occurs but the unexpected often does.

No-one knows how the day will end.

Nothing happens by accident or chance.

Tomorrow do thy worst, for I have lived today.

Don't envy the sinner – who knows what awaits him.

Where you live determines who you are.

Three coincidences are no coincidence.

The fault, dear Brutus, is not in our stars,
But in ourselves . . .

Shakespeare

The moment makes the man.

One person's loss is another person's gain.

In hindsight things always seemed inevitable.

"All I could do was play the cards I was dealt," said the loser.

FAULTS

Faults are thick when love is thin.

We suspect in others the faults we could commit ourselves.

We are often liked more for our faults than for our virtues.

There are some whose faults become them.

Don't tell a person his faults – he may cure them but not forgive you.

We may learn more from our faults than our virtues.

I prefer friends with faults to those without.

All affectations are faults.

Quarrels would not last so long, if the fault was only on one side.

If youth is a fault, then it's soon cured.

It's hard to forgive someone who has no faults.

The faults in others are enjoyable because they reflect our own.

We recognise in others that which
we hide from ourselves.

When love fails, we see all the faults.

Marriage helps us appreciate our faults.

By confessing small faults, we give the impression we have no large ones.

A fault confessed is half redressed.

If we had no faults, we would have no friends.

If we had no faults, we would find no enjoyment in the faults of others.

FAVOURS

Never claim as a right what you can get as a favour.

Doing favours is not the best way of winning friends.

Knowing how to refuse a favour is a very useful art.

What starts as a favour can end up as a right.

To accept a favour is to give one.

Don't lose a friend by too many favours.

Never forget a favour received
or remember favours given.

One way or another you always pay for a favour.

There is no such thing as a free lunch.

Milton Friedman

We don't quite forgive the giver.

Never let those under you do you a favour
– it will cost you dear.

FEAR

If it were not for fear, sinning would be enjoyable.

In extreme fear we revert to childhood.

Fear cannot be without hope – or hope without fear.

Fear comes from uncertainty.

Fear preserves life.

Repentance is not so much remorse as fear of the consequences.

It is safer to be feared than loved.

In moments of crisis, fear is blocked out.

Who causes fear cannot be free from fear.

It is the unhappy people who fear change most.

The things we desire are often more dangerous than the things we fear.

Vows made in fear are soon forgotten.

What we don't understand we fear, and what we fear we hate.

Remove the fear and you remove the power.

Our worst fears are those that never happen.

It was fear that first brought God into the world.

Fear is the product of the imagination.

With a guilty conscience, you live with fear.

The less we know, the more we suspect.

A good fright is the best advice.

When we get frightened, we look for scapegoats.

Guilt and fear are cousins.

Curiosity will conquer fear,
even more than bravery will.

Fear is stronger than love.

It is fear or hopes which make beliefs.

A tyrant doesn't mind being hated – as long as
he is feared.

The wolf doesn't fear the dog but his bark.

Fear is the parent of cruelty.

How easily fear can turn into hate!

Don't fear the weapon – fear the man.

Prejudice is the fear of something different.

The anticipation of pain can
be worse than the pain itself.

We often make jokes about things that frighten us.

Desire is another form of fear.

Ships fear fire more than water.

Flattery

Flattery is a device for theft.

If we did not flatter ourselves, there would be few pleasures left.

To ask advice is usually to seek flattery.

Flattery is the food of fools.

If you can't love, you must learn to flatter.

Imitation is the highest form of flattery.

Flatterers look like friends, the same way as wolves look like dogs.

Those who flatter you more than usual have either deceived you or wish to.

What flatters a person is the thought
that he is worth flattering.

By flattery you can get people to do good.

None is safe from flatterers.

He who knows how to flatter you will know how to slander you.

A flatterer is a person who tells you your opinion and not his.

Mark Twain

Vanity is the greatest of all flatterers.

If you want the daughter, flatter the mother.

We often praise others, in the hope
of being praised ourselves.

Beware of the person who speaks well of everyone.

The best way to entertain some people
is to listen to them.

FOOLS

Fools are wise as long as they remain silent.

Thanks to fools we may appear wise.

The tongue of the fool is his damnation.

Bible

Even the fool – when he holds his tongue
– is considered wise.

The fool may ask questions that the wise
cannot answer.

He who knows he's a fool is not a great fool.

Say nothing and they might think you a fool – say something and they will know you are.

A fool may give a wise man counsel.

If fools wore crowns, we would all be kings.

Be wise and hear – be a fool and speak.

If it weren't for fools, the rest would not succeed.

Without the company of fools, a witty person would be lost.

Ridicule is the first and last argument of a fool.

To laugh at a fool is one way of being one.

Flattery is the food of fools.

We are all a little foolish but wisdom consists of not exceeding that limit.

Dreams lift up fools.

A learned fool is sillier than an ignorant one.

By the law of averages, fools must be right sometimes.

Success makes a fool seem wise.

The wise can play the fool but the fool cannot play the wise.

To live without a little foolishness is not as wise as you think.

The wise may change his mind but the fool never will.

A fool will always find someone more foolish to advise him.

Fools do eventually what the wise do at once.

We all play the fool once – to marry is to play it always.

Most fools only think they are ignorant.

The bigger the fool, the louder the laughs.

Drink and money make wise men fools.

Children and fools have merry lives.

Fools live poor to die rich.

Talk sense to a fool and he'll call you foolish.

To be a fool at the right time is a great art.

To laugh at the wise is the privilege of the fool.

Though a fool may try to act wise he is still a fool.

A drunk will be sober next day but a fool will still remain a fool.

Wise men walk while fools sleep.

"The Duke sometimes can be a perfect fool," said the Duchess. "Nobody's perfect," said Alice.

Passions turn wise men into fools.

A hero is a fool who doesn't tell any one how afraid he is.

FORBIDDEN

Forbidden fruits taste sweetest.

Adam didn't want the apple for the apple's sake but because it was forbidden.

We long for the forbidden thing and desire that which is denied us.

Forbid something and it becomes desirable.

FORGIVENESS

To know all is to forgive all.

Whoever does you a bad turn won't forgive you.

It's hard to forgive a giver.

To forgive easily is to invite insults.

To forgive is to gain a victory. √

Forgive others but not yourself. √

The offender never forgives.

Consider this your last day and you'll be √ ready to forgive.

We may forgive injuries but not contempt.

Forgive them for they know not what they do.

Jesus

If they can't repay you, they won't forgive you.

Pardon the offence and you will encourage more.

Beware of the person who does not return your blow – he will not forgive you or allow you to forgive yourself.

Bertrand Russell

A tyrant may forgive his subjects for not liking him – provided they don't like each other.

It's hard to forgive someone who has no faults.

Confess to God and you'll be forgiven – confess to man and you'll be laughed at.

It is the confession, not the priest, that gives absolution.

The robbed that smiles steals something from the thief.

Shakespeare

No person can truly condemn another, because no person really knows another.

Every sin can be absolved.

Though your sins are many, they are forgiven because you have loved much.

Jesus

Don't tell a person his faults – he may cure them but not forgive you.

We don't quite forgive the giver.

Let he who seeks revenge dig two graves.

Chinese saying

Revenge keeps your own wounds green.

Fortune

We can bear our friends' misfortune better than we can bear their good fortune.

With bad fortune we blame fate – with good we credit our own cleverness.

An ounce of fortune is worth more than a sack of gold.

Misfortune tells us what fortune is.

Bad fortune will soon lose you friends.

Even the unlucky need luck.

Many blessings come in disguise.

The shoe that pinches one may fit another.

What good is beauty without fortune?

Everything comes to the person who doesn't need it.

Weep for the man who doesn't know his good fortune.

Confucius

The peach was once a bitter almond.

Fortune comes in many disguises – including calamity.

Who has no ill fortune is troubled with good.

Freedom

Freedom means responsibility – that's why we most dread it.

Freedom is no more than a chance to do better.

None but the beggar can really be free.

What atrocities are committed in the name of freedom!

No-one is perfectly free until all are free.

Man is born free but everywhere is in chains.

Rousseau

Forgetfulness is a form of freedom.

The slave has one master – the ambitious has many.

Freedom means the right to be disliked.

Freedom to starve is no freedom at all.

Some suppress freedom in the name of law and order.

The greatest release is the release from love.

Tyranny is always better organised than liberty.

Revolution is the right of the slave.

It is often safer to be in chains than to be free.

How much more freedom you may have, once you
have lost your reputation.

Freedom is a light for which many men
have died in darkness.

George Washington

"Freedom" is just another word for
"nothing left to lose".

FRIENDS

Everybody's friend is nobody's friend.

Sudden friends lead to repentance.

You are known by the friends you keep.

Old friends are best friends.

Those over-friendly may be cheating you.

There is no greater relief than to escape
from a half friend.

The strongest bond of friendship is a mutual enemy.

If we could read their thoughts, our friendship would
soon end.

A mirror will tell you what your friends will not.

The misfortunes of our friends are not wholly
displeasing to us.

Ready money is our best friend.

If you want to keep a friend, better not test him.

Treat your friends as if one day they may turn foe.

If we had no faults, we would have no friends.

Doing favours is not the best way of winning friends.

To get rid of a friend, lend him money.

Don't run yourself down – your friends will
do that for you.

In prosperity, our friends know us – in adversity, we know our friends.

To get rid of a friend, tell him something for his own good.

The best way to find a friend is to be one.

Distance helps to keep our friends near.

I prefer friends with faults to those without.

A rich person is not short of friends.

Make a person feel important and you make a friend.

We cherish our friends, not for their ability to amuse us, but for our ability to amuse them.

To be liked by everyone is to be loved by none.

Success has many friends.

Your friend has a friend – so tell no secrets.

My enemy's enemies are my friends.

A friend in power is a friend lost.

It is not the lack of love but the lack of friendship that ends marriage.

The rich never know who their friends are.

Why end a beautiful friendship by marriage?

Wealth makes many friends.

Business brings money – but friendship hardly ever does.

Keep your friends close and your enemies closer.
Sicilian saying

Better to lose a jest than to lose a friend.

No-one really minds seeing a friend fall off the roof.
Mark Twain

Better to have a good enemy than a bad friend.

Two fighting dogs become allies when a wolf comes along.

Make friends of your clients and not clients of your friends.

FUTURE

The future often arrives before we are ready for it.

The future is a mirror without glass.

Yesterday was our past; today is our future because tomorrow is unknown.

No-one knows how the day will end.

The atomic age is here to stay – but are we?

There's not much future in being old.

The anticipated seldom occurs – but the unexpected often does.

Life is a long preparation for something that never happens.

W B Yeats

We all think we are immortal – until we reach forty.

Gambling

Gambling is the best way to get nothing for something.

Those who gamble pick their own pocket.

When you gamble you share with the devil.

Gamble to lose – don't gamble to win.

Gambling is an illness with no cure.

No bookmaker thinks gambling is a mug's game.

Betting is the argument of a fool.

Money won is twice as sweet as money earned.

Slow horses and fast women have been many
a man's downfall.

We may win in the beginning but lose in the end.

Fate deals the cards.

The winner is the person who knows when to quit.

I backed the right horse but the wrong horse won.

"All I could do was play the cards I was dealt,"
said the loser.

GIVING

They give twice who give quickly.

No-one is impoverished by giving.

The more you give, the more you will get back.

The way you give is more important than the gift.

Small gifts make friends – a great one
will make an enemy.

The great tragedy of poverty is not knowing the luxury of giving.

The beggar does more for the giver than the giver for the beggar.

The sinner who spends and gives is better than the miser who hoards.

When we enjoy giving, then giving
is no longer a virtue.

We can't afford to have things given us.

Lend before witnesses but give without them.

It is better to give than to receive.

Cast your bread upon the waters
and it will be returned.

Bible

It is annoying to give to a beggar
and it is annoying not to.

The person who gives little with a smile gives more than the person who gives more with a frown.

It's good to give – but not too much.

GOD

Where God is, there is no loneliness.

God hides things by putting them near.

Who searches for God has already found Him.

God will forgive – that is His business.

At night, an atheist half believes in God.

Take one step towards God and He'll take two steps towards you.

God loves the poor but helps the rich.

Prayer doesn't change God – but it changes us.

Woman was God's second blunder.

Suicide is God's gift to man.

We may change our faith, without changing our God.

Danger past – God is forgotten.

A doubter might come closer to God than all the churchgoers.

A lot of people are leaving the church and going back to God.

To believe in God makes life so much easier.

If God doesn't exist, everything is permissible.

Dostoevsky

How lucky to believe in God
– without the burden of religion.

Evelyn Waugh

Government

A society of sheep will be governed by wolves.

Bad officials are elected by good citizens who don't bother to vote.

Bureaucracy is a giant mechanism run by pygmies.

Public office is the last refuge of incompetence.

Oscar Wilde

A government who robs Peter to pay
Paul will always get the support of Paul.

The successful revolutionary is a statesman
– the unsuccessful one is a criminal.

Leadership does not depend upon being right.

Gratitude

Be grateful for the beggar – he gives you the chance to feel superior.

Nothing is more degrading than to be eternally grateful to someone.

Being grateful is often a wish to obtain more benefits.

Be grateful for pain – it shows you are alive.

If you can't be grateful for what you have got, be grateful for what you have not got.

Gratitude buys nothing.

Gratefulness is the poor man's payment.

Gratitude is one of the secrets of happiness.

A blind man won't thank you for a mirror.

The worse the journey, the sweeter the arrival.

Save a thief from the gallows and he will live to cut your throat.

After ingratitude, gratitude is hard to bear.

Thanks to fools, we may appear wise.

Thank heaven for hypocrites – they keep the arts going.

Mark Twain

Kindness done grudgingly is not worth thanking. ✓

GREATNESS

A man is great only when he is kneeling.

Pope Pius X

The price of greatness is responsibility.

A man is as big as his decisions.

Churchill

The strongest person is he who stands alone.

Most great men are usually bad.

There would be no great people
if there were no small people.

To be great is to be misunderstood.

Nothing great was ever achieved without enthusiasm.

True greatness requires retaining
the simplicity of a child.

History is the biography of great men.

There are no great criminals – only great crimes.

GREED

Greed grows by what it feeds on.

Greed and desperation know no limits.

We mistake greed for ambition.

Greed is the driving force of industry.

Without greed there would be no progress.

Appetite comes with eating.

Pleasures are spoilt by wanting more.

Our tragedy is not what we have but what we want.

The more we have, the more we want.

Discontent arises more from our desire than our needs.

We give up one pleasure only for a greater one.

An obsession to increase wealth
is a main source of misery.

We never know what is enough – until we have had more than enough.

Too good may be too bad for us.

Three good meals a day is bad living.

Overeating is digging your grave with your teeth.

Ambition is really only hidden greed.

Envy is passive greed.

The less you expect, the more chance
of happiness.

Buddha

GUILT

A guilty person runs when no-one is chasing.

The guilty make excuses before being accused.

How much unnecessary sadness is caused by guilt!

A sense of guilt goes with excess pleasures.

There is no guilt from which we cannot be absolved.

The sense of guilt instilled by religion is a main destroyer of happiness.

Those who shout the loudest usually
have the most to hide.

Guilt and fear are cousins.

The things we condemn are the things we are capable of ourselves.

Giving presents may suggest guilt.

If you are angry, the chances are you might be in the wrong.

To deny your guilt is to double it.

Who strikes first admits he is wrong.

The guilty are their own executioner.

Explaining is half confessing.

The troubles we bring on ourselves are often the hardest to bear.

Churchgoers are no better than others
but suffer more guilt.

Too many people spend their lives choking on guilt.

The greatest pain is that which is self-inflicted.

There is luxury in self-reproach.

Guilt is the scar of our childhood.

The damage done by guilt is crippling.

People use guilt to manipulate us.

How satisfying to feel guilty when you have done nothing wrong.

Guilt goes hand-in-hand with pleasure.

Guilt activates our stress hormones.

We need scapegoats to purge ourselves of our own guilt.

HAPPINESS

You are always punished for too much happiness.

Happiness is not a right – except for children.

The less we understand, the happier we may be.

Happiness always seems just out of reach.

The more sensitive we are, the less chance we have of being happy.

Happiness is a station between too little and too much.

To be happy we should not concern ourselves too much about others.

Excess happiness may be harder to bear than sorrow.

The search for happiness is one
cause of unhappiness.

To chase after happiness is to run from contentment.

The happiest people often seem to be the ones with least reason for being so.

Happy the person with a short memory.

You won't be happy if you think too much.

The bird of happiness goes to the hand that does not try to grasp it.

Confucius

Happiness and sorrow are close relatives.

The malicious have a dark happiness.

Too much happiness is dangerous.

Hope is the greatest happiness we may allow ourselves.

Happiness is the interval between unhappiness.

Lack of memory is often essential for happiness.

To describe happiness is to diminish it.

Happiness is often nothing more than good health and poor memory.

What we call happiness is what we don't know.

Happiness is liking what you do
and doing what you like.

There is a lot of happiness
in having what others cannot.

Happiness is being able to admire without desiring.

Happiness always comes too late.

The greatest of all happiness is to know you are loved.

One secret of happiness is gratitude.

Don't confuse money with happiness.

You are not happy, unless you think you are.

We have no right to expect happiness, unless we have earned it.

Happiness vanishes when envy appears.

Beauty is the promise of happiness.

From happiness to sorrow may take a moment. From sorrow to happiness may take years.

"When I start feeling happy I ask myself, 'Where's the catch?' " said Alice.

Not everyone who laughs is happy.

Happiness is not wanting for anything.

Buddha

Imagination may not make us wise
but it may make us happy.

To mourn for someone you loved could be happiness.

Puritanism is the fear that someone may be happy

The Puritan's main impulse is to punish those with a greater capacity for happiness than he has.

You don't know what happiness is until you get married – then it's too late.

Pleasure is the beginning and the end of living happily.

Better to be happy than to be wise.

Happiness is just being happy.

You can live happily if you spread some happiness – a pleasure shared is twice as pleasing.

The world's a happy place for a fool.

Happiness belongs to those who think of others.

For us to be happy it's not only necessary that we must succeed but perhaps also that others must fail.

To be without some of the things you want is an indispensable part of happiness.

Bertrand Russell

There is something rather boring about somebody else's happiness.

Money can't buy happiness but only the rich say that.

Only the fool is really happy.

The more refined one is, the less chance of happiness.

One road to happiness is acceptance.

The happy do not believe in miracles.

HATE

Hate is the coward's revenge for being frightened.

A great hate may give a purpose to life.

Love blinds us to people's faults but hate blinds us to their virtues.

We hate those who make us feel inferior.

The greatest hate often springs from the greatest love.

Nobody hates a proud man more than another proud man.

If you knew this was your last day,
would you still hate?

If you hate yourself, you can love no other.

Prejudice is the maximum hate
for the minimum reason.

Hatred is by far the longest pleasure.

Lord Byron

Strong hates reveal our secret desires.

Misery generates hate.

You will hate in a person that which is part of yourself.

How easily fear can turn into hate.

HELL

One road to paradise – many to hell.

A fool's paradise is a wise man's hell.

Hell is where heaven is not.

The road to hell is paved with good intentions.

Hell is not as bad as the road that leads to it.

Adam was the first to enter hell.

Endless pleasure is a definition of hell.

Better to go to heaven in rags than to hell in finery.

HISTORY

The history of civilisation is the history of barbarism.

History is little more than a register of crimes, follies and misfortunes.

History is mostly guessing and prejudices – men who make history have little time to write it.

War makes good history but peace makes poor reading.

The only thing we learn from history
is that we don't learn.

The past cannot be altered – except by historians.

Happy is the country whose history is boring.

History might be useful if it were true.

History is a set of lies agreed upon.

History is the study of other people's mistakes.

History proves war is better at abolishing nations than nations at abolishing war.

We are tomorrow's past.

In all ages hypocrites called priests have put crowns on the heads of thieves called kings.

History is a catalogue of things which should
not have happened.

History is the biography of great men.

History is what we decide afterwards.

In great events no-one is a prophet until it happens.

Today's terrorists are tomorrow's presidents
– look at history.

History is always written by the victors.

Hope

Hope is the last gift given to man.

Hope is the greatest happiness we may allow ourselves.

Hope carries us pleasantly through life.

Hope is the poor man's bread.

Hope is merely putting off disappointment.

Hoping may be better than having.

Hoping and waiting turn wise men into fools.

Patience is the art of hoping.

While there is hope, there's hope.

Extreme hopes are born from extreme miseries.

Often the most unreasonable hopes have been the cause of great success.

It is good to hope but foolish to depend on it.

To give up hope is to give up life.

While we feel shame, there is hope for us.

Vows begin when hope dies.

Ignorance gives the possibility of hope.

Poverty is not being without money
but being without hope.

Hope is as cheap as desire.

Fear cannot be without hope – nor hope without fear.

No-one is so old that he doesn't hope
to live a little longer.

Justice is a hope and not a certainty.

We are all in the gutter, but some of us are looking at the stars.

Oscar Wilde

The rest of your life starts tomorrow.

The best is yet to come.

Life begins the other side of despair.

"I'll see you in paradise," said my friend.

When it is dark enough, you can see the stars.

The miserable have no other medicine
But only hope.

Shakespeare

Jesus said to the thief on the cross,
"Today you will be with me in paradise."

In my end is my beginning.

Mary Queen of Scots

Better to travel hopefully than to arrive.

There is always sunshine somewhere in the world.

The first shall be last and the last shall be first.

Bible

To hope for paradise is to live in paradise.

You may be down but not out.

An unhappy poor man hopes money will help him – an unhappy rich man has not that hope.

If Winter comes, can Spring be far behind?

Shelley

The peach was once a bitter almond.

He who only hopes is hopeless.

Out of the strong shall come forth sweetness.

Bible

Freedom is a light for which many men have died in darkness.

George Washington

You may be broke but you don't have to be poor.

Hope is an expensive emotion.

There is no certainty without hope.

HUMAN NATURE

The meanness of the rich is as surprising as the extravagance of the poor.

Most of us enjoy the inferiority of our friends.

When we are afraid, we say we are cautious – when others are, we say they are cowards.

As long as war is looked upon as wicked, it will have its fascination.

We recognise in others that which we hide from ourselves.

We all have mob self and individual self in us.

Self-interest is the root of human behaviour.

"Do we respond more readily to fear of punishment or hope of reward?" asked Alice.

We can bear our friends' misfortune better than we can their good fortune.

We may forgive a person but still not trust him.

The things we condemn are the things we are capable of ourselves.

It's natural to resent those who have helped us.

Every king needs a jester.

No-one is totally good or totally bad.

We may feel sympathy for their suffering but find it hard to feel pleased at their pleasures.

The devil is an optimist if he thinks he can make people meaner than they are.

If you want to know what a man is,
place him in authority.

Man is not a logical creature but an emotional one.

Inferiors revolt that they may be equal and equals revolt that they may be better.

Voltaire

Snobbery is one of the great driving forces in society.

People aren't just a little corrupt – corruption is a progressive disease.

Everyone is more or less mad every now and then.

No-one can hurt you as much as you can hurt yourself.

It's not your looks but your deeds
that make you human.

Superstition is part of being human.

Men are not naturally good.

Machiavelli

HUMANITY

It is easier to love humanity as a whole than to love your neighbour.

It is through pity that we remain human.

We may excuse an inhuman act by saying we are merely human after all.

It is not how you look but how you act
that makes you human.

It is our failures that make us human.

The atomic age is here to stay – but are we?

In Flanders fields the poppies blow
Between the crosses row on row.

John McCrae

Every beggar is descended from some king
– and every king from some beggar.

If we were all naked, how could we tell who
were the kings?

All wars are civil wars because we are all brothers.

What price can we pay for our soul?

Bible

Who weeps for others remembers himself.

There are no illegitimate children
– only illegitimate parents.

A single death is a tragedy – a million deaths a statistic.

An ale house won't harm a good person – and a church
won't benefit a bad one.

We are all descended from Adam.

Through suffering we have consciousness.

If fools wore crowns, we would all be kings.

Pain has no favourites.

You may do an evil thing without being evil.

You can't be a hero without being a coward.

We are our own worst enemy and dig our own grave.

Jesus wept.

Bible

Art is the first sign of civilisation.

Our true nationality is humanity.

No human being is of great importance.

Plato

Everyone is naked under their clothes.

HUNGER

Hunger is the best sauce.

Hunger drives the wolf from the forest.

Hunger is the best physician.

A warm welcome is the best meal.

Fasting can be a good tonic.

The Lord sends the food and the devil sends the cook.

Dry bread at home is better than a feast abroad.

You don't have to be a cook to enjoy the meal.

Appetite comes with eating.

Hypocrisy

Be a hypocrite but don't talk like one.

Thank heaven for hypocrites – they keep the arts going.

Mark Twain

A humanitarian is often a hypocrite.

A hypocrite who always acts the same way ceases to be one.

Nothing is more unpleasant than a virtuous person with a mean mind.

The usual pretext of those who make us unhappy is that they do it for our own good.

To pretend to be wicked but really doing good would be a form of hypocrisy.

Oscar Wilde

Always speak your mind – even if you don't mean it.

Mark Twain

He's a saint away but a devil at home.

Hating gossip ourselves, we are grateful for those who do it.

Saki

A patronising disposition usually has its mean side.

Too much modesty is conceit.

To enjoy a good reputation, give publicly and steal privately.

Servants are the biggest snobs of all.

Virtue is so praiseworthy, we often practise
it out of self-interest.

We wish respect from others even though we may not respect ourselves.

In all ages hypocrites called priests have put crowns on the heads of thieves called kings.

If you can fake sincerity, you can fake anything.

Laurence Olivier

When is betrayal not betrayal? When it is business.

Hypocrisy is prejudice with a halo.

It's appearance, not truth, that counts.

Machiavelli

IDLENESS

Idleness is a vocation.

Jerome K Jerome

Idleness, though inexcusable, is man's true state.

Few people have enough character to be idle.

Jerome K Jerome

It takes contentment to be idle.

Everyone is or hopes to be an idler.

It's not easy to convince a busy person that it is better to be idle.

Idle people have the least leisure.

An idle youth makes a needy old age.

The devil tempts all, but an idle person tempts the devil.

It is impossible to enjoy idling thoroughly unless one has plenty of work to do.

Jerome K Jerome

Tomorrow is the busiest day of the year.

Spanish saying

None but the beggar can really live at ease.

I have no time to be in a hurry.

Jerome K Jerome

How much harm is caused by the belief
that work is honourable.

A learned man is an idler who kills time by study.

George Bernard Shaw

It takes character to stand the rigours of idleness.

Beau Brummell

Time being idle is never wasted.

Lazy people have no spare time.

IGNORANCE

Ignorance leaves the possibility of hope.

Ignorance is the peace of life.

Ignorance is the enemy of art.

Ignorance is essential to make life bearable.

Some ignorance is required for happiness.

An argument is an exchange of ignorance.

It is impossible to defeat an ignorant person
in an argument.

"I have never met a person so ignorant I could
not learn something from him," said Alice.

The little I know, I owe to my ignorance.
George Bernard Shaw

Superstition is the religion of the ignorant.

Out of ignorance comes fear.

Through ignorance we keep innocence.

Beware of those whose ignorance is joined with piety.

Most fools only think they are ignorant.

The beginning of knowledge is to know
we are ignorant.

The less we know, the more we suspect.

False knowledge is more dangerous than ignorance.

Aggression is the last resort of the ignorant.

The ignorant person always prefers the things he
cannot understand.

Oh, what comfort there is in ignorance!

A wise ignorance is an essential part of knowledge.
Plato

ILLUSIONS

Illusion is more attractive than reality.

The illusion of pleasure is the reality of life.

Avoid reality – illusions are better.

Nothing is sadder than the death of an illusion.

Don't part from illusions – they keep us from suffering too much.

Fooling ourselves a little helps us on our way.

The unobtainable is the most desirable.

Our real life is often the one we do not live.

The past looks better than it was
– only because it's not here.

We are such stuff as dreams are made on.

Shakespeare

Drink makes a person better pleased with himself if not better pleased with others.

Illusion is the first of the pleasures.

IMAGINATION

Imagination is more important than knowledge.

Imagination may not make us wise but
it may make us happy.

Imagined pleasures are sweetest.

Imagination is the first step to believing what isn't.

What is now proved was once imagined.

Imagination is the better part of enjoyment.

Fear is the product of the imagination.

It is more tantalising to conceal than reveal.

If you have no imagination, you will have no pity.

A great part of love is in the imagination.

IMPORTANCE

A cockerel is very important on his own dunghill.

Having power is the ability of not having to please.

A lot of things don't matter very much – and most things don't matter at all.

The people who think themselves important are the first to have breakdowns.

The graveyards are full of indispensable men.

IMPRESSIONS

First impressions are half the battle.

A person may be very secretive, yet have no secrets.

What may be mistaken for shyness may be plain selfishness.

A silent person tells us something.

Good clothes will open many doors.

First impressions last.

INJUSTICE

Injustice may sometimes be bearable – it's justice which may not.

Injustice is the only blasphemy.

Who pardons the bad injures the good.

Extreme justice is extreme injustice.

The pleasures of the rich are the tears of the poor.

Minor thieves are hanged – major ones are honoured.

The rich man keeps cool in the summer – the poor man in the winter.

A single death is a tragedy – a million deaths a statistic.

You always flog the willing horse.

Soldiers win battles – the generals get the credit.

In law you ruin yourself twice – once when you lose and once when you win.

One person's misfortune is another's good fortune.

To the jaundiced, all things are yellow.

Humour has to have a victim.

An injury to one is an injury to all.

A man is as old as he feels – a woman as old as she looks.

When you are right no-one remembers
– when you are wrong no-one forgets.

All profit is unjust to someone.

Where is justice if we fail to punish the guilty?

INNOCENCE

Innocence is no protection.

The price of knowledge is the loss of innocence.

Who increases knowledge increases sorrow.

The truly innocent are those who think others so.

To the pure, all things are pure.

St Paul

Oh, for the innocence of our childhood! Sadly we get wiser every day.

To believe in goodness and decency,
we must have innocence.

Through ignorance we keep innocence.

Innocence needs protection and should be hidden.

Childhood is a kingdom where nobody dies.

A child's world is much nicer than the real one.

They are rich whose pleasures are cheapest.

When all the world is young, lad . . .
And every lass a queen.

Charles Kingsley

Children at play are not playing
– their games are real.

Innocence is a man's weakness but a child's strength.

What has once been learned cannot be unlearned.

Beauty must have a touch of innocence.

Money can't buy back your innocence.

Unless you become as little children you shall not enter the kingdom of heaven.

Jesus

Credulity is man's weakness but the child's strength.

Oh, to retain the simplicity of a child!

Innocence is part of childhood.

Only a child's life is a real life.

IRONY

Selfishness often seems a quality that inspires love.

Men who cherish the highest respect for women seldom seem popular with them.

If you want to ruin someone's reputation, don't speak ill of them but praise them highly.

People are seldom attracted to us by our doing them kindness.

The less you do, the more tired you get.

Through failure we may possibly succeed.

Giving in may sometimes be the best way to succeed.

Many make themselves poor by trying not to appear poor.

Some people with great virtues are disagreeable, while others with great vices are quite agreeable.

To try to forget something is the sure way of thinking of nothing else.

We may accept great misfortunes, yet resent small ones.

We seldom live long enough to profit from our mistakes.

A woman will not forgive a man for the sacrifices he makes on her account.

Those who love most are often the least valued.

Sometimes a piece of bad luck can come in very handy.

Where there is too much, there is something missing.

Some have been thought brave because they had not the courage to run away.

The greatest crimes are often caused by having too much rather than too little.

Men tire themselves in pursuit of leisure.

We are often intolerant in support of tolerance.

The tortoise wins the race while the hare is sleeping.

There are times when to apologise is to be rude.

The finest amusements are often the most pointless ones.

A woman will start a row, then ask you to apologise.

Only through violence may brutality sometimes be ended.

The operation was a success but the patient died.

A nation is only at peace with itself when it is at war.

The hardest work is doing nothing.

Money often stops you getting the things you want.

How much harm may be done by doing good!

It is often safer to be in chains than to be free.

By the time we make it in life, most of us are past it.

With the clowns come the tears.

Everyone's responsibility is no one's responsibility.

Men rattle their chains to show they are free.

We are not satisfied with being right, unless we can prove the other was wrong.

Jealousy

Jealousy is a great exaggerator.

Love is blind – but jealousy sees too much.

Moral indignation is jealousy in disguise.

To love without some jealousy is not true love.

Few of us can stand other people's prosperity.

Nobody hates a proud man more
than another proud man.

When a proud man hears another praised, he thinks himself injured.

The most primitive and elemental cause of violence is sexual possessiveness.

Judgment

Judge people by their questions rather
than their answers.

If Jack's in love, he is no judge of Jill's beauty.

First impressions are half the battle.

There is a time to see and a time to look away.

Onlookers see more than the players.

Let he who is without sin cast the first stone.

Jesus

Who overvalues himself will undervalue others.

Hate the sin and not the sinner.

A wrinkle on a man is considered experience – on a woman, age.

No person can truly condemn another because no person really knows another.

The present is judged by the past.

JUSTICE

Justice is a hope and not a certainty.

Justice may be too good for some and not good enough for others.

Injustice may sometimes be bearable – it's justice which may hurt.

Extreme justice is extreme injustice.

Success may blind us to justice.

There are some acts of justice which corrupt those who perform them.

The price of justice is eternal publicity.

Much law but little justice.

Who harms others harms himself.

Death is the great leveller.

The guilty are their own executioner.

Conscience is its own punishment.

Truth is its own witness.

Examine the contents and not the bottle.

It is not the colour of the skin but of the mind that counts.

Pain has no favourites.

The first winner may be the last loser.

The suffering of the rich is among the sweetest pleasures of the poor.

Who causes fear cannot be free from fear.

If we are not punished for our crimes, why complain if we are not rewarded for our virtues?

Self defence is no offence.

Charity to the deserving is not charity but justice.

Justice in the abstract is a fairly meaningless concept.

Where is justice, if we fail to punish the guilty?

KINDNESS

Kindness may be the most unkind thing of all.

Kindness is in our power but fondness is not.

A kindness done grudgingly is not worth thanking.

It is easier to be kind to people we care little for.

You can still be kind to people without really liking them.

People are seldom attracted to us by our doing them kindness.

You can do wrong to people but too much kindness is also dangerous.

No act of kindness is ever wasted.

One can cope with a lot of things except sympathy.

No more goodness should be attempted than people can bear.

Where truth does harm – then tell white lies.

Most kindness is doubtful.

You don't have to be kind but you must appear to be.

Knowledge

Knowledge grows with doubt.

Knowledge does not teach us wisdom.

In much knowledge is much sorrow.

Bible

What use is knowledge, if no-one knows you have it?

The price of knowledge is the loss of innocence.

The pursuit of knowledge is often more satisfying than its assimilation.

To know all is to forgive all.

Who knows much, suffers much.

Only the shallow know themselves.

Oscar Wilde

The beginning of knowledge is to know we are ignorant.

Mediocre people often have the most acquired knowledge.

False knowledge is more dangerous than ignorance.

What use is knowledge without wisdom?

Faith is the belief without evidence.

Imagination is more important than knowledge.

Those who know little often repeat it.

The little I know, I owe to my ignorance.

George Bernard Shaw

Knowing is not the same as understanding.

A learned fool is sillier than an ignorant one.

The more we know, the more we realise
we don't know.

No person is worse off for knowing the worst
about himself.

"The older I get, the less I know," said Alice.

Through adversity we know ourselves.

The more we know, the less we believe.

We differ from all other creatures because we know we
are mortal.

Thinking is not the same as knowing.

All that I really know is that I know nothing.

Socrates

I regret not knowing earlier what I know now.

Tony Benn

In hindsight things always seemed inevitable.

If I had known I was going to live so long I would have
taken better care of myself.

W Somerset Maugham

First rule of victory – know your enemy.

Fear comes from uncertainty.

What is now proved was once imagined.

We are all in the gutter – but some don't know it.

What has once been learned cannot be unlearned.

Knowledge does not rest only on truth but
also on error.

Knowledge is strength because forewarned is forearmed.

You can pass on knowledge but not wisdom.

The simplest questions may be the hardest to answer.

Doubt is the key to knowledge.

Knowing how to refuse is as important as knowing
how to accept.

A little knowledge is dangerous, but no knowledge is
even more so.

A wise ignorance is an essential part of knowledge.

Plato

Better to hide your knowledge than show
your ignorance.

Laughter

Laughter is the finest tonic.

Laughter is the cheapest luxury we can enjoy.

Laughter often has a touch of cruelty.

Laughter is a tranquilliser with no side effects.

Laughter reduces blood pressure.

Laughter may be a defence mechanism.

Laugh now – cry later.

To laugh at a fool is one way of being one.

A day without laughter is a wasted day.

We laugh sometimes that we may not weep.

We are here for a short time – let's get all the laughter we can.

It is hard to dislike someone who makes you laugh.

The bigger the fool, the louder he laughs.

What we laugh at reveals our character.

To make people laugh, you must remain serious.

Not every laugh is a happy one.

Laughter may signify anger.

To laugh at the wise is the privilege of the fool.

There are more votes in making people laugh than in making them think.

Humour has to have a victim.

A maid that laughs is soon taken.

Better to smile last than to laugh first.

He who laughs has not yet heard the bad news.

We are the only species with the gift of laughter – let's use it!

Make someone laugh and you've got a friend.

Laughter changes the chemicals of the brain and releases stress.

Laughter is the shortest distance between two people.
Victor Borge

When a person is not amused, he feels contempt for those who are.

What is funny to one person is an insult to another.

LAW

It is better to know the judge than to know the law.

The law never made a person more honest.

In law the only certainty is the expense.

In law you ruin yourself twice – once when you lose your case and once when you win it.

The more laws, the more offenders.

Go to law for a sheep and you will lose your cow.

Necessity has no laws.

A lawyer never goes to court himself.

Much law but little justice.

Win your case and lose your money.

A good denial is the best point in law.

One lawyer makes work for another.

Men are not hanged for stealing horses, but that horses may not be stolen.

Lord Halifax

LEARNING

We may learn more from our faults than our virtues.

If you don't learn from the past, you will repeat it.

A great deal of learning can be packed into an empty head.

No person becomes wise just from learning.

The most learned are not always the most wise.

The wise will learn from everyone.

Marriage is a school where one learns too late.

Through doubt we may learn.

Lessons are not given, they are learnt.

"I have never met a person so ignorant I could not learn something from him," said Alice

Perhaps we may only learn through failure.

Give instructions to the wise and they will be yet wiser.

Prejudice comes with learning.

The most learned people are often the most boring.

To teach is to learn twice.

Children love to learn but hate to be taught.

The scars of others should teach us caution.

Failure teaches us that we will probably fail again.

A learned man is an idler who kills time by study.

George Bernard Shaw

If something is learned quickly, it is usually forgotten quickly.

Learning is sometimes a convenient way of not having to think.

Listen to the fool – you may learn something.

The only thing we learn from history is that we don't learn.

You can learn more from failure than you can from success.

LENDING

Lend only what you can afford to lose.

Who lends loses twice.

To lend is to buy a quarrel.

By lending you could make an enemy.

To get rid of a friend, lend him money.

Better to give ten than to lose twenty by lending.

Lend before witnesses but give without them.

If they can't repay you, they won't forgive you.

Creditors have better memories than borrowers.

Lending to a person makes him lose his memory.

If you have no money to lend, you won't make an enemy.

LIES

I much prefer a lying compliment to a sincere criticism.

Oscar Wilde

The cruellest lies are those told in silence.

A clever liar does not go into details.

A big lie is often more plausible than the truth.

Those who will lie for you will lie against you.

I don't mind lying but I hate inaccuracies.

Oscar Wilde

One lie makes for many.

A forgetful liar is a sad sight.

You can tell if someone makes a mistake
but not if they are lying.

Those who don't need to lie are proud
of not being liars.

I do believe her, though I know she lies.

Shakespeare

A little inaccuracy saves a lot of explaining.

Who serves two masters must lie to one.

A half truth is a whole lie.

It takes a clever person to lie well.

There is no greater lie than a truth misunderstood.

The best lies are the short ones.

When someone is very polite, he is probably lying.

History is a set of lies agreed upon.

A good liar makes a little lie go far.

It is easier to believe strangers because they have not yet deceived us.

Pretend to believe a liar – he will then lie even more and reveal himself.

How badly a person lies when you know he is lying.

The greater the lie, the greater the chance
of it being believed.

A believable lie is better than a stupid fact.

Italian saying

If truth does harm, then tell white lies.

Being nice to people is often another way of lying.

When someone says they don't mind,
it usually means they do.

If a child tells a lie, don't call him a liar
– tell him he has told a lie.

The art of living is knowing how to believe in lies.

We are born truthful but die liars.

LIFE

Life is a process of endless decay.

Life begins the other side of despair.

Life is the art of being deceived.

Life would be bearable if it were not for its pleasures.

Life is short but troubles make it long.

Life is a battlefield and we are all walking wounded.

Regret for yesterday and fear for tomorrow are the tragedies of life.

When life appears to be treating you well – watch out!

Our real life is often the one we don't live.

To waste time is not to have discovered
the value of life.

Death is an extension of life.

If we realise life's shortness, we may cease to hate.

Anger and temper will shorten life.

The rest of your life starts tomorrow.

To give up hope is to give up life.

If we spoke the truth, life would be even
more unbearable.

We are born a king – but die in exile.

All animals except man know the purpose
of life is to enjoy it.

Everything changes – nothing changes.

The fairest silk is stained first.

The most beautiful bird gets caged first.

Youth is a blunder – manhood a struggle
– old age a regret.

I have wasted time – now time has wasted me.

Goethe

It is a mistake trying to be more agreeable than you really are.

Most of us spend the first part of our life making the remainder miserable.

In the midst of life we are in death.

Bible

There is no cure for birth or death but to enjoy the interval.

In good company the journey is short.

The shoe that pinches one may fit another.

You may live long but get little out of life.

One day there will be no tomorrow.

The days are too long but life is too short.

Look for the ridiculous in everything and you'll find it.

One cloud is enough to darken the sky.

We crucify ourselves between two thieves – regret for yesterday and fear for tomorrow.

Bertrand Russell

If you think you are going mad, you must be sane.

Joseph Heller's *Catch 22*

The first breath is the beginning of death.

Life would be impossible without a sense of humour.

Life is what happens to you while you are making plans.

Most people deserve better.

By the time we make it in life, most of us are past it.

A useless life is an early death.

Nice guys finish last.

Life is a long preparation for something
that never happens.

Without dreams, how unbearable life would be.

"If anybody has discovered the secret of life, don't tell
me – I don't want to know," said the Duke.

A great hate may give a purpose to life.

If you don't think about death, you won't
appreciate life.

So much of our life is wasted in loneliness.

The illusion of pleasure is the reality of life.

Variety may be the spice of life but it is also the
complication of life.

The art of life is in the avoidance of the unobtainable.

Ignorance is essential to make life bearable.

We spend the first half of our life collecting things and
the second half trying to get rid of them.

The most important time of one's life is now
– right now.

Tony Curtis

Living

Living well is the best reward.

Try to live as if this was your last day.

The art of living is knowing how to believe in lies.

Try to live every day of your life.

We are all living a life of quiet desperation.

George Bernard Shaw

We don't live as we like to but as we have to.

It's not how we die but how we live that counts.

We can live like a lord yet die like a fool.

Most of us exist but do not live.

The art of living is knowing how far to go
– then to go a little further.

He lives long who lives well.

To live in someone's heart is not to die.

Death is God's last gift to the living.

Three good meals a day is bad living.

Better to live rich than to die rich.

If you have lived properly, you will have made plenty of mistakes.

We cried when we were born – and now we know why!

It's not how long we live but how well we live.

The longer you live, the sooner you'll die.

The more you live in the past, the less
you live in the present.

Anyone can live like a millionaire for five minutes.

Aneurin Bevan

All decent people live beyond their incomes nowadays – and those who are not respectable live beyond other people's.

Saki

Be grateful for pain – it shows you are alive.

I've paid a high price for living so long.

W Somerset Maugham

LONELINESS

Loneliness makes strange bed fellows.

Loneliness robs us of our happiness
and mocks our success.

Loneliness cannot be described,
it can only be experienced.

No-one is so lonely as he who loves only himself.

What fools call loneliness, the wise call solitude.

If you don't like loneliness, then don't marry.

Where God is, there is no loneliness.

Be good and you'll be lonely.

Being on your own is not the same as being lonely.

The captain is the loneliest man on the ship.

Lonely people get to believe what suits them.

Being alone in paradise would be hell.

So much of our life is wasted in loneliness.

What good is love without someone to love?

You may have everything yet have nothing.

Prayer is the need to be heard.

You can be lonely on your own but even lonelier with the wrong person.

LOVE

Love is a great exaggerator.

Love blinds us to reason.

Love is a disease few have a cure for.

Love unspoken is love denied.

Love is blind but jealousy sees too much.

Love can't take advice and lovers won't.

Love makes time pass and time makes love pass.

Love is the wisdom of the fool
and the folly of the wise.

Samuel Johnson

Love conquers all. (*Amor vincit omnia.*)

Love a little less but a little longer.

Hot love is soon cold.

The first sign of love is the last sign of wisdom.

Pity is the sweetest form of love.

A fence between makes love more keen.

A great part of love is in the imagination.

'Tis better to have loved and lost
Than never to have loved at all.

Alfred Lord Tennyson

Each man kills the thing he loves.

Oscar Wilde

To doubt the power of love is to doubt everything.

When love fails we see all the faults.

One should always be in love – that's why no-one should ever get married.

Oscar Wilde

The English love – the French make love.

Parents love for what they give
– children for what they receive.

To love without some jealousy is not true love.

If it wasn't for love, there would be less divorces.

If you love yourself, at least you will have no rivals.

Regret is dead but love remains.

Alfred Lord Tennyson

The lack of love is the greatest sin.

Those who love most are often the least valued.

You can choose to begin love – but not to end it.

A great love is seldom returned.

A short absence quickens love – but a long one kills it.

In her first passion a woman loves her lover,
In all the others all she loves is love.

It is very sad to be in love with someone who doesn't love you – but far worse to be loved by someone you no longer love.

Christianity has done a great deal for love –
by making a sin of it.

Free love may be love but it is not free.

We are blinded by love but our eyes
are opened by marriage.

Love ceases to be a pleasure once it ceases to be secret.

A woman will despise a man for loving her unless she can return his love.

To have never been loved is to have never lived.

Your sins are forgiven because you loved much.

Jesus

To try to analyse love is to diminish it.

Love is a form of insanity.

Make love, not war – but both can kill you.

Love eventually dwindles into convenience.

Many a heart is caught on the rebound.

If you can't have what you love, you must love what you have.

If you can't love, you must learn to flatter.

Faults are thick when love is thin.

LUCK

Courage and skill are worth little without luck.

Even the unlucky need luck.

You are lucky when you know you are lucky.

If you eat a toadstool and don't die, it was a mushroom.

Shallow people believe in luck.

Better to have luck than money.

The harder you work, the luckier you get.

Beauty is better than luck.

"Bad luck may sometimes be good luck in disguise.
Think about it," said Alice.

If you have luck, you don't have to be perfect.

"In the long run," said Alice,
"everything depends on luck."

MAN

Man hands down misery to man.

Man is the only animal that blushes, or needs to.

Mark Twain

Man is a make-believe animal – his dreams are his hopes.

Our true nationality is mankind.

We are all descended from Adam.

Every man at heart is a bachelor.

Oscar Wilde

All creatures have their natural enemies – man is everyone's.

The atom bomb has changed everything except our thinking – thus we are drifting towards catastrophe.

Einstein

It was a man's world until the arrival of Eve.

Man is the only creature that consumes without producing.

A man is led the way he wishes to follow.

We are all descended from apes.

We are the only species with the gift of laughter
– so let's use it!

It's language that marks us out from all other creatures.

Only man is self-important, therefore only man
can be ridiculous.

MANNERS

Good manners are made up of petty sacrifices.

Good manners mean behaving yourself more
than necessary.

Oscar Wilde

Good manners consist in concealing how much we
think of ourselves and how little we think of others.

Mark Twain

Good manners cost nothing but are worth everything.

Good manners are lost in poverty.

Bad manners spoil everything – even reason and justice.

It is bad manners to silence a fool – and cruel to let
him go on.

The test of good manners is to be patient with
bad ones.

Being a gentleman is a disadvantage these days.

Prosperity often breeds bad manners.

When someone says they don't mind – it usually means they do.

I don't really want people to be very agreeable to me – as it saves me the trouble of being very agreeable to them.

Jane Austen

I was as civil to him as his bad breath would allow me.

Oscar Wilde

MARRIAGE

Marriage is the best way to end a beautiful friendship.

Marriage is the last refuge of the impotent.

Oscar Wilde

Marriage has two days of happiness – the first day and the last.

Marriage is a school where one learns too late.

Marriage is a romance in which the hero dies in the first act.

Mae West

Marriage is a grounds for divorce.

Marriage is a great institution but I'm not ready for an institution just yet.

Mae West

One should always be in love – that's why one should never get married.

Oscar Wilde

For an ideal marriage the man should be deaf and the woman blind.

It's not the lack of love but the lack of friendship that ends marriage.

Honest men marry soon – wise men never.

Don't marry for money – just fall in love
where money is.

Who marries for money earns it.

If you don't like loneliness, then don't get married.

You marry when you grow up – but how do
you know when you've grown up?

We are blinded by love but our eyes
are opened by marriage.

We all play the fool once – to marry
is to play it always.

To marry once is a duty; to marry twice is a folly;
to marry three times is madness.

Oscar Wilde

When a young man marries, he divorces his mother.

Who marries a widow and three children
marries four thieves.

You don't know what happiness is until you get
married – then it's too late.

The prospect of a contented widowhood keeps many a wife hopeful.

Honeymoon for a month – trouble for life.

Every man at heart is a bachelor.

Oscar Wilde

Fire and flame for a year – ashes for the remainder.

After the wedding it is too late for regret.

Always look at the mother before you marry the girl.

Marriage is the only adventure open to the coward.

Voltaire

I married beneath me – all women do.

Nancy Aster

Only women should get married.

Oscar Wilde

An obedient wife rules her husband.

MEMORIES

Save us from our memories.

The things we remember are those best forgotten.

The indiscretions of our youth are the happy memories in our old age.

Happy the person with a short memory.

The weather was always fine in happy memories.

We may shut out realities but not memories.

Bygone troubles are sweet to remember.

Forgetfulness is a form of freedom.

Forgetfulness helps ease our grief.

The wound may heal but the scar remains.

To try to forget something is the sure way of thinking of nothing else.

If we could not forget, we would not be free from grief.

Eaten bread is soon forgotten.

The promises of the night are forgotten at daybreak.

Even the bad times were good.

Lending to a person makes him lose his memory.

Oh! To have the days of our childhood restored or be able to forget them.

Obsession with the past can ruin our future.

Dangers past – God is forgotten.

Can you remember the worries of a year ago?

I'll see you again whenever spring breaks through again.

Song

What has been is past forgetting.

Pain is forgotten when gain follows.

Age, like distance, lends enchantment.

For the sake of auld lang syne.

Robert Burns

"I would be a very happy person," said Alice, "if it wasn't for my memories."

Better to forget than to remember and regret.

If you tell the truth, you don't have
to remember what you said.

"Memories, memories! Please spare me from memories," said the old man.

In the mist of a memory you wander back to me.

Memories are always rosier than the reality.

MISERS

Misers are kind people – they leave
their wealth for others.

A rich miser is poorer than a poor person.

The sinner who spends and gives is richer than the miser who hoards.

The man who dies rich dies in disgrace.

Andrew Carnegie

It is stupidity to live poor and die rich.

You may live long but get little out of life.

The use of money is better than its possession.

The more money you have, the harder
it is to part with.

Misfortune

Misfortune hastens age.

Misfortune tells us what fortune is.

Our worst misfortunes are often those that
never happen.

We may accept great misfortunes yet resent small ones.

The end of one misfortune is a step nearer the next.

The fear of misfortune is often greater than the
misfortune itself.

One person's misfortune is another's good fortune.

How much easier to accept the misfortunes of others.

Remembering our misfortunes gives
us an added misfortune.

Who has no ill fortune is troubled with good.

Bad fortune will soon lose you friends.

Our misfortunes are sometimes a blessing in disguise.

The heaviest baggage is an empty purse.

One cloud is enough to darken the sky.

Even to lose may be some gain.

Sometimes a piece of bad luck can come in very handy.

Many a person's misfortunes have kept him out of jail.

We can bear our friends' misfortune better than we can bear their good fortune.

The misfortunes of our friends are not wholly displeasing to us.

MODERATION

It's not the drinking that's to blame but the excess.

Too little does not satisfy – too much spoils.

Happiness is a station between too little and too much.

Too much courtesy is discourtesy.

MONEY

Money is something you need in case
you don't die tomorrow.

Money often costs too much. ✓

Money is the sixth sense that helps us
enjoy the other five.

Money might buy a good dog ✓
– but not the wag of its tail.

Money won is twice as sweet as money earned.

Money doesn't just talk – it sings.

Money is neutral. It's what you do with it that counts.

You will always find money for the devil.

The more money we have, the harder it is to part with.

Jack would be a gentleman if he had money.

To be clever enough to get plenty of money you must be stupid enough to want it.

All the money in the world won't buy an extra minute of time.

When it comes to money, enough is never enough.

If a person is happy, what can money buy him?

Ready money is our best friend.

Who marries for money earns it.

Don't marry for money – just fall in love where money is.

The price we pay for money is our freedom.

I'd like to live like a poor person with plenty of money.

Pablo Picasso

A heavy purse is light to carry.

The trouble with being rich is having to mix with other rich.

With a full purse you won't be short of friends.

Gold dust blinds all eyes.

"All the money I save, I spend," said Paddy.

If you are disagreeable but have money, they will call you an eccentric.

It must be great to be rich and not to
have to keep up appearances.

Whoever is rich is my brother.

Greek saying

Money can't buy back your innocence.

An unhappy poor man hopes that money will help him
– an unhappy rich man has not that hope.

You can't be too thin or too rich.

Duchess of Windsor

Money can't buy happiness
– but only the rich say that.

A billion dollars is not what it used to be.

Paul Getty

If it wasn't for women, money
would have little meaning.

Aristotle Onassis

Money has no smell.

MORALITY

Morality is moral only when it is voluntary.

Morality is merely a matter of time and geography.

Morality is the herd instinct in the individual.

Nietzsche

The test of morality is what you
do when you have power.

Moral indignation is jealousy in disguise.

When Puritans moralise they call it duty.

An immoral person is someone
who is enjoying himself.

How many vices or virtues are really very important?

Injustice is the only blasphemy.

Don't confuse opinions with principles.

Chastity is the most unnatural of all perversions.

Bertrand Russell

Who serves two masters must lie to one.

"My morality is this," said Alice.
"I ask myself who does it hurt?"

Without a victim, how can there be a crime?

The Nuremberg defence: "I was just obeying orders."

Immorality is not new but it now
seems more acceptable.

What is natural cannot be immoral.

Nietzsche

NECESSITY

Necessity leaves us no choice.

Necessity knows no laws.

Necessity will never make a good bargain.

Necessity relieves us of decision making.

Necessities grow with want.

When luxuries grow, so do necessities.

The luxuries of yesterday are the necessities of today.

One is vain by nature but honest by necessity.

Virtue is often a matter of necessity.

Hunger drives the wolf from the forest.

Necessity does the work of courage.

Necessity is the argument of tyrants.

NEIGHBOURS

We are told to love our neighbours and our enemies – probably because they are the same people.

It may be easier to love humanity
as a whole than our neighbours.

Love your neighbour but choose your neighbourhood.

What the neighbours might think stops
us doing many things.

If you want good neighbours, build a high fence.

Good neighbours are those you never see.

When your neighbour's house is on fire, try not to
show too much pleasure.

Your neighbour's apples always look sweetest.

NOSTALGIA

Our todays may be tough but our yesterdays were great!

All times past were good.

There is no greater sadness than remembering
happy days past.

What a wonderful life I've had
– if only I'd realised it sooner.

Judy Garland

The past looks better than it was,
only because it is not here.

What was hard to endure is sweet to recall.

O! Call back yesterday, bid time return.

Shakespeare

Sweet childish days, that were as long
As twenty days are now.

William Wordsworth

For the sake of auld lang syne.

Robert Burns

It was always summer in our childhood.

The more you live in the past,
the less you live in the present.

OBSERVATIONS

Better to weep with the wise than
laugh with the fool.

Better to regret your silence once than your words
many times.

Better to play the fool a little than to be thought a
complete fool.

Better to appear stupid like the others than appear
clever like none.

Better to smile last than to laugh first.

Better to ask many times than to get lost once.

Better to break the engagement than
to break the marriage.

Better to have a plain wife for yourself than a beautiful
wife for others.

Better to be happy than to be wise.

Better to hide your knowledge than
to show your ignorance.

Better to go to heaven in rags than to hell in finery.

Better to travel hopefully than to arrive.

Better to die a beggar than live a beggar.

Better to break than to bend.

Better to wear out than to rust out.

Better to give ten than lose twenty by lending.

Better to suffer a great evil than to do a small one.

Better to flatter the devil than to fight him.

Better to die in honour than to live in shame.

Better to lose a jest than to lose a friend.

Better to be embarrassed than to be ashamed.

Better to go away longing than to go away loathing.

Better to be disliked for what you are than to be liked for what you are not.

Better to sleep without supper than to rise in debt.

Better to live one day as a lion than a hundred years as a sheep.

Better to go begging than to go stealing.

Better to cut the shoe than to pinch the toe.

Better to die on your feet than to live on your knees.

Better to be envied than to be pitied.

Better to arrive late than not at all.

Better to sleep on a wooden bed than to lie in a golden coffin.

Better to waste your youth than to do nothing with it.

Better to be born lucky than to be born rich.

Better to die of good wine than of bad illness.

Better to be alone than in bad company.

Better to have a just war than an unjust peace.

Better to turn back than to go wrong.

Better to make a weak man your
enemy than your friend.

Better to love less but love longer.

Better to keep the devil at the door than turn him out of the house.

Better to love too much than to love too little.

'Tis better to have loved and lost
Than never to have loved at all.

Alfred Lord Tennyson

Better to give than to receive.

Better not to show your teeth if you can't fight.

Better to light a candle than curse the darkness.

Better to take caution at first than to have tears later.

Better to be good than pious.

Better to have an ugly truth than a beautiful lie.

Better to have a hundred enemies outside the house than one inside.

Better to be an old man's darling
than a young man's fool.

Better to know the judge than the law.

OLD AGE

Old age is but an extension of childhood.

The tragedy of old age is not that we are old but that we are young.

You are getting old when people start saying how well you look.

To grow old is to pass from passion to compassion.

A person may be old at thirty or young at eighty.

None of us is so old we don't hope
to live a little longer.

We would like to live long but not to grow old.

A man is as old as he feels
– a woman is as old as she looks.

A man is as old as the woman he feels.

You never realise how you have aged until you see an old photograph.

Few of us know how to grow old.

There is not much future in being old.

Truth looks different as we get older.

Youth lasts longer than we think
– it's old age that's unexpected.

The old give advice because they can no longer give example.

Old men become children for the second time.

Men never grow up – their toys just get bigger.

"The older I get, the less I know," said Alice.

Age will accomplish what talent has failed.

A smile will make you look ten years younger.

Wisdom may increase with age but so does folly.

Age, like distance, lends enchantment.

Darling, I am growing old – silver hair among the gold.
Song

Don't worry about avoiding temptations – as we grow old they avoid us.

The years go by so quickly – it is the days that are long.

We are never old in our dreams.

A drink makes the old young.

Old men are dangerous because they no longer care what will happen to the world.

Old age is always ten years ahead.

The old often survive the young.

Have ideals in your youth because
you won't in old age.

If you have lived properly, you will have made plenty of mistakes.

The things we regret are the things we did not do.

One day there will be no tomorrow.

It is loss of interest – not age – that makes you age.

Ageing is when a woman looks in the mirror and suddenly sees her mother.

Wrinkles on a man are considered experience – on a woman, age.

Grow old along with me!
The best is yet to be.

Robert Browning

Don't begrudge growing old – many are
denied the privilege.

Try to die young at a very old age.

If I had known I was going to live so long I would have taken better care of myself.

W Somerset Maugham

"Why the black tie?" asked Alice.
"I'm in mourning for my lost youth," said the Duke.

"Thinking is the one excitement now left,"
said the old man.

OPINIONS

When we ask for an opinion we are merely seeking approval.

Nothing is more conducive to peace of mind than having no opinions at all.

Mark Twain

Don't confuse opinions with principles.

A flatterer is a person who tells you your opinions and not his.

Mark Twain

Conscience is often conforming with the opinions of others.

"I have no politics or religion – just opinions," said Alice.

Shyness is often the result of having too high an opinion of yourself.

Isn't it annoying to be wrong when you know you are right?

Mark Twain

Being sincere does not mean being truthful.

Belief is often a matter of taste.

Those who don't change their opinions love themselves more than they love truth.

The minorities are sometimes right.
The majorities never.

George Bernard Shaw

Opinions are a result of emotions rather than thinking.

Our enemy's opinion of us may be the truth.

Only strong characters can be influenced – the weak ones know it all.

Prejudice is an opinion without judgment.

Convictions are more dangerous enemies of truth than ideas.

OPPORTUNITY

Opportunity makes the thief.

We only do what we want – given the choice.

Being thought witty allows us a greater opportunity to play the fool.

The follies we regret are those we did not commit when we had the opportunity.

The moment makes the man.

Two dogs fight over a bone – the third one gets it.

Many a person would be a rogue if he knew how.

When the lights are out, the mice will dance.

You won't get a six if you don't throw the dice.

If we make no mistakes we make nothing.

It is the thought of what we have missed that makes our sadness.

How sad the words, "It might have been."

There are two types of men: those who have committed adultery and those who wish they had.

You never know what you might have done if you had been tempted.

Freedom is no more than the chance to do better.

In the land of the blind the one-eyed man is king.

Many a person is saved from being a thief by finding everything locked up.

Opportunity is picking the right moment
for grasping a disappointment.

Next to knowing when to seize an opportunity, the most important thing is knowing when to forego an advantage.

OPTIMISM

Hope carries us pleasantly through life.

The optimist is always broke.

Nothing great was ever achieved without enthusiasm.

The prospect of a contented widowhood keeps many a wife hopeful.

Famous last words: "I bet this gun isn't loaded."

Beyond the clouds the stars still shine.

"What shall we do now?" asked the tortoise.
"Count our blessings," said Alice.

PARADISE

The poor will have the best seats in paradise.

Being alone in paradise would be hell.

Jesus said to the thief on the cross, "Today you will be with me in paradise."

"I'll see you in paradise," said my friend.

A fool's paradise is a wise man's hell.

The keys to the gates of paradise also
open the gates of hell.

One road leads to paradise – many lead to hell.

A Jug of Wine, a Loaf of Bread – and Thou
Beside me singing in the Wilderness –
Oh, Wilderness were Paradise enow!
Edward Fitzgerald – *Omar Khayyám*

It is not necessary to make a hell of this world
to enjoy paradise in the next.

To hope for paradise is to live in paradise.

Contentment is the nearest we will get to paradise in this world.

The beautiful leads to the eternal.

Gold opens most doors, except heaven's.

Having the least desires takes us to paradise.

Unless you become as little children,
you shall not enter the kingdom of heaven.

Jesus

Heaven holds a place for those who pray.

Paradise is man's easiest invention.

PARADOX

The meanness of the rich is as surprising as the extravagance of the poor.

Kindness may be the most unkind thing of all.

To make people laugh you must remain serious.

It is easier to carry two buckets of water
than to carry one.

If only I could get a hangover
I wouldn't drink so much.

Richard Burton

The closer you are, the less you can see.

Sometimes the best gain is to lose.

Error itself may be a happy coincidence.

The first winner may be the last loser.

The happiest people often seem the ones with the least reason for being so.

Those who are always unhappy often seem proud of the fact.

To mourn for someone you loved could be a happiness.

"Bad luck may sometimes be good luck in disguise. Think about it," said Alice.

PASSIONS

All passions have a touch of sadness.

Passions kill reason and accept prejudice.

Passions turn wise men into fools.

The end of passion is the beginning of repentance.

It is easier to avoid passions than to control them.

Serving our passions is the greatest slavery.

It is surprising how much vitality love can produce.

What is spoken from the heart is usually a lot lower down.

The greatest hate often springs from the greatest love.

PAST

The present is only the continuation of the past.

We are all tomorrow's past.

The past cannot be altered except by historians.

Yesterday was our past; today is our future because tomorrow is unknown.

The present is judged by the past.

To live for the moment is not to deny the past.

Those who don't remember the past are condemned to repeat it.

All times past were good.

Obsession with the past can ruin our future.

PATIENCE

Patience is the art of hoping.

Slowly slowly catchee monkey.

Burmese saying

If we went slower, we might get there sooner.

Haste has been the downfall of many.

Take one day at a time.

Patience is despair disguised as virtue.

Don't shoot yourself five minutes before the reprieve.

The test of good manners is to be patient with bad ones.

Patience is the only remedy for poverty.

Penalty

The hard thing about success is having
to keep being a success.

Every sin brings its own punishment.

No genius is free from a touch of madness.

Evil has a sweet beginning but a bitter end.

Serving our passions is the greatest slavery.

Depend on others and you'll never get fed.

Punishment follows excess.

The borrower is servant to the lender.

The pursuit of pleasure is not without pain.

Pain is the price you pay for loving.

People

People are never more ridiculous than when they take
themselves seriously.

People are seldom attracted to us by our
doing them favours.

I drink to make people bearable.

Richard Burton

Weak people, when united, become strong.

All charming people are spoiled – that's the secret of their charm.

Oscar Wilde

I don't really want people to be very agreeable to me – as it saves me the trouble of being very agreeable to them.

Jane Austen

Every person is important to himself.

A wise person knows things
– a shrewd person knows people.

There would be no great people if there were no small people.

There is no saint without a past or sinner without a future.

We are all descended from Adam.

It is surprising how nice people can be when they know you are leaving.

Woe to the one no-one likes – but beware of the one everyone likes.

Most great men are usually bad.

Some people never stop to think – others never think to stop.

I've always been interested in people but I've never really liked them.

W Somerset Maugham

A person appears to you the way you appear to him.

The wisest person can fool himself.

Cheerful people can be just as annoying
as miserable ones.

There is a very fine line between genius and madness.
Aristotle

There is no such thing as a bad person – only a person acting badly.

Most people deserve better.

For many people, being involved in violence is the most exciting thing they do.

Even a president must have a private life.
Bill Clinton

Solemn people are generally humbugs.

PITY

Who pities others remembers himself.

It's through pity that we remain human.

In our pain we have no pity for others.

Don't give pity – give action.

Beware of pity.

If you have no imagination, you will have no pity.

The world is full of troubles but we can only feel our own.

PLEASURES

Pleasure is the beginning and the end of living happily.

Pleasure is seldom found where it is looked for.

Pleasures are spoilt by wanting more.

Pleasures imagined are sweetest.

The pleasures of the rich are the tears of the poor.

The pursuit of pleasure soon bores.

Endless pleasure is a definition of hell.

Short pleasures bring long repentance.

Life would be bearable if it wasn't for its pleasures.

There is no pleasure without some pain.

They are rich whose pleasures are cheapest.

A sense of guilt goes with excess pleasures.

We often pay dearly for our pleasures.

Anticipation is the better part of pleasure.

It is the chase and not the catch that gives the greatest pleasure.

We tire of the pleasures we take but not of those we give.

If we did not flatter ourselves, there would be few pleasures left.

There is pleasure in the pursuit of anything.

I conceal the unhappiness in my life
by buying pleasures.

Barbara Hutton

We give up one pleasure only for a greater one.

Suffering is real – pleasures are imagined.

Beauty is that which pleases.

The greatest pleasures are often the most pointless ones.

The price we pay may ruin our pleasure.

Visitors always give pleasure – if not on their arrival, then on their departure.

A lot of our guilt is a morbid way of looking at our pleasures.

Illness is often the price we pay for pleasure.

Hatred is by far the longest pleasure.

Lord Byron

What pleasure it would be if only we could say what we thought.

Illusion is the first of the pleasures.

Wealth is not a lot of pleasure by itself – it must be shown off to be enjoyed.

Don't suffer in silence – it takes the pleasure out of it.

Guilt goes hand-in-hand with pleasure.

Puritans take their pleasures sadly.

Pleasure is heightened by guilt.

Love ceases to be a pleasure once it ceases to be secret.

You can live happily if you spread some happiness – any pleasure shared is twice as pleasing.

Imagined pleasures are sweetest.

POSSESSIONS

Possessions are usually diminished by possessions.

The joy of possession seldom lasts.

You may have everything yet have nothing.

Where there is too much, there is something missing.

Too many people are ruined by too much.

Our tragedy is not what we have but what we want.

The larger the roof, the more snow it collects.
Russian saying

With riches come worries.

A golden key opens most doors.

Only beggars are really free.

The only difference between the toys of the young and the toys of the old is the price.

Golden shackles are worse than iron ones.

Gandhi

If you have one watch you know the time – if you have two you are never sure.

In the land of the blind, the one-eyed man is king.

The more you have, the more you have to lose.

By having nothing we have everything.

Buddah

POVERTY

Poverty is no shame, but being ashamed of it is.

Poverty was created to give the rich
opportunity for charity.

Poverty makes handsome women ugly.

Poverty is feeling poor.

Poverty is not being without money
but being without hope.

Good manners are lost in poverty.

In poverty you have no power.

The great tragedy of poverty is not knowing the luxury of giving.

When poverty enters the door, love leaves
by the window.

The worst form of poverty is to be in debt.

God loves the poor but helps the rich.

A rich miser is poorer than a poor person.

The rich can't imagine poverty.

By having nothing we have everything.

Buddha

Charity is no cure for poverty.

I'd like to live like a poor person with plenty of money.

Pablo Picasso

Hope is the poor man's bread.

They that envy are always poor.

An empty purse fills the face with wrinkles.

The devil dances on an empty purse.

Anything will fit a naked man.

The rich keep cool in the summer
– the poor in the winter.

To have no butter for your bread
is not complete poverty.

If you are poor, you will have no fear of being robbed.

The greatest poverty is being unwanted.

Patience is the only remedy for poverty.

Poverty is not the sin of the poor but the sin of the rich.

Just pretending to be rich has kept many poor.

"Poverty keeps together more families than it breaks up," said Alice, knowingly.

Only the poor can feel for the poor.

POWER

Power is the ultimate aphrodisiac.

Kissinger

Power corrupts a few but weakness corrupts many.

Power can be more important than profit.

Power is not wisdom.

The test of morality is what you do when you have power.

The reputation of power is power.

Women don't realise the power of their flirtations.

Put a uniform on a man and power goes to his head.

A friend in power is a friend lost.

If a person has no delicacy, he has you in his power.

Having power is the ability of not having to please.

You can get further with a kind word and
a gun than with a kind word alone.

Al Capone

A loaded gun beats a royal flush.

It doesn't worry the fox the number of sheep there are.

Without power, try to act brave.

Henchmen can become worse than their masters.

Getting really indignant helps to harness your power.

Leadership does not depend upon being right.

If you want to know what a man is,
place him in authority.

To hurt some you must have power over them.

The greater the power, the greater the abuse.

Power is a most precious drug.

PRAYER

Prayer is the need to be heard.

Prayer is in your heart and not on your knees.

Prayer doesn't change God but it changes us.

Prayer is better than sleep.

Confucius

Who prays for others will be heard for himself.

When the gods wish to punish us they answer our prayers.

When prayers are not answered that could be the answer.

To want to pray is to pray.

To love well is to pray well.

Who enjoys the most prays the most.

Back on shore we pray no more.

Life is fragile – treat it with prayer.

Protect us from what we want.

God doesn't listen to the prayers of the proud.

Prayer works because it works.

Heaven holds a place for those who pray.

I close my eyes so I might see.

St Augustine

Everyone has a need to confess.

A man is great only when he is kneeling.

Pope Pius X

PREJUDICE

Prejudice is the reasoning of fools.

Prejudice is the maximum hate for the minimum reason.

Prejudice is an opinion without judgment.

Prejudices are a short cut to thinking.

From prejudice to barbarism is but a single step.

We reveal our character in our prejudices.

We use reason to justify our prejudices.

We are tribal animals and prejudices are natural.

Passions kill reason and accept prejudice.

Our prejudices are our masters.

Through education we get a higher grade of prejudice.

I am free from prejudice – I dislike everyone equally.

W C Fields

Those who have no convictions are the most prejudiced.

Often when we think we are thinking we are merely rearranging our prejudices.

Differences breed prejudices.

Hypocrisy is prejudice with a halo.

Common sense consists of the prejudices laid down in our youth.

Environment and conditioning are brothers to prejudice.

It is not the colour of the skin but the colour of the mind that matters.

What we don't understand we fear,
and what we fear we hate.

Dogma is the end of thought.

We are all prisoners of our experience.

Where there is no common language there is suspicion.

There is no such thing as a pure race.

Examine the contents and not the bottle.

All our blood is the same colour.

Nationalism is the disease of mankind.

No-one is born with prejudice.

Prejudice is the fear of something different.

Racism is not a way of thought
– it is an absence of thought.

PREVENTION

An ounce of prevention is worth a pound of cure.

Being bored is sometimes the price for keeping out of trouble.

A stumble may prevent a fall.

It is easier to avoid passions than to control them.

It is the second word that makes the quarrel.

A wise person does not need a weapon.

No-one can make you feel inferior without
your consent.

PROFIT

In all labour there is profit.

Bible

All profit is unjust to someone.

We seldom live long enough to profit
from our mistakes.

There is no gain without pain.

We only profit at the expense of others.

One person's loss is another's gain.

Power can be more important than profit.

Everything we do is done with an eye
to something else.

Many receive advice but how many profit from it?

The best way to profit is through others' folly.

PUNISHMENT

Failure is not the only punishment
but the success of others.

Anger punishes itself.

When the gods wish to punish us they
answer our prayers.

The worst punishment is a sleepless night.

Distrust all those in whom the desire
to punish is powerful.

Nietzsche

We often pay dearly for our pleasures.

Punishment always follows excess.

Who harms others harms himself.

It's hard to be efficient without being unpopular.

If you deceive others, you also deceive yourself.

If you dig a pit you might fall into it.

Bible

Cowards die many times before their deaths.

Shakespeare

Shame follows pride.

Humiliation is the biggest revenge of all.

Threaten someone with a greater punishment and he
will accept a smaller one willingly.

The doctrine of an eye for an eye leaves everyone blind.
Martin Luther King

The way to punish someone is to grant all their wishes.

Reality

We may shut out reality but not memories.

The reality is hardly ever as pleasant as the imaginary.

Avoid reality – illusions are better.

Fantasy is better than reality.

To dream is happiness – to wake is reality.

Food, warmth and shelter are the essentials – the rest, to some degree, is luxury.

Only the truth really hurts.

In our pain we have no pity for others.

We weep for the beauty that could be and the horrors that are.

Socrates

Expectation is the better part of realisation.

It is good to hope but foolish to depend on it.

Fooling ourselves a little helps us on our way.

We dislike many things in order
not to dislike ourselves.

What attracts us to someone seldom binds us to them.

If we said what we thought, life would be unbearable.

An iron chain or a silk cord can both imprison.

You can't fill your purse with dreams.

We all live by selling something.

If our parents had not been tempted,
we would not be here.

What is spoken from the heart is usually
felt a lot lower down.

Try to be reasonable and it will be taken for weakness.

The light at the end of the tunnel may be the light of
an oncoming train.

There never was a golden age.

Only through violence may brutality sometimes
be ended.

Sometimes the best gain is to lose.

Marriage kills romance.

We only impress ourselves.

Everything is free – until you come to pay for it.

Free offers always come with a price tag.

Without greed there would be no progress.

The optimist is always broke.

We don't always wish to hear the truth.

Many kiss the baby for the sake of the nurse.

A man doesn't comfort a pretty widow
just out of kindness.

Every day stupid people say things that are not stupid.

Vows begin when hopes end.

Go to law for a sheep and you will lose your cow.

The art of living is the avoidance of the unobtainable.

Freedom means responsibility
– that's why most dread it.

A blind man won't thank you for a mirror.

Once something has been invented
it cannot be disinvented.

Don't fear the weapon – fear the man.

The icing is great – but where is the cake?

Fantasy can't disappoint – only reality can.

It is hard to bear too much reality.

What use is a sundial at night?

Anticipation is worse than the reality.

By the law of averages, fools must be right sometimes.

REGRET

Regret is dead but love remains.

Alfred Lord Tennyson

To regret deeply is to start afresh.

We often regret the good we have done
as much as the ill.

The follies we regret are those we did not commit
when we had the opportunity.

More have regretted through speech than
through silence.

I regret not knowing earlier what I know now.

Tony Benn

The temptations resisted in our youth are the ones we
regret the most.

Talk long enough and you will regret.

We would often be sorry if our wishes were granted.

After it is done it is too late for advice.

Anger nearly always ends in regret.

After the wedding it is too late for regret.

Regret for yesterday and fear for tomorrow are the
tragedies of life.

The things we regret are the things we didn't do.

You get wise from listening and regret from speaking.

REPUTATION

To enjoy a good reputation, give publicly
and steal privately.

Respect is greater at a distance.

If you want to ruin someone's reputation, don't speak ill of them but praise them highly.

Get the reputation of being a wit and lose the reputation of being sensible.

The reputation of power is power.

The reputation of being honest is more important than being honest.

How much more freedom you may have once you have lost your reputation.

What is a person but his reputation?

Every great artist has been helped by being dead.

RESENTMENT

Cynics are only contented when making the world as barren for others as they have for themselves.

Familiarity in a superior is resented because it cannot be returned.

We may be less upset by our own poverty than by the wealth of others.

Nothing is more degrading than being eternally grateful to someone.

Nothing is more annoying than someone with less intelligence but more sense than us.

Virtue is praised but disliked.

Puritans hate blood sports – not for the animals' sake
but because it gives pleasure to the hunters.

RESULTS

Remove the cause and you will remove the effect.

Every light will have its shadow.

A small spark may burn down a forest.

A drop of poison will ruin the barrel.

There is no gain without pain.

A boiling kettle will overflow.

We are the result of our thoughts.

If you lie with dogs, you will rise with fleas.

Misery generates hate.

If you play with the devil, you will end up in hell.

You are always punished for too much happiness.

If you laugh when you borrow,
you will cry when you repay.

What starts as a favour ends up as a right.

It is the last drop that makes the overflow.

The first winner may be the last loser.

By trying to persuade others we convince ourselves.

REWARD

The hope of reward sweetens labour.

Love is the reward for love.

Virtue is its own reward.

Living well is the best reward.

The reward for having done something well is having done it.

The reward for success is success.

He lives long who lives well.

The worse the journey, the sweeter the arrival.

The more you give, the more you will get back.

Who prays for others will be heard for himself.

Pain is forgotten when gain follows.

No rest is worth having, unless it follows work.

There are many paths to the top of the mountain – but only one view.

No-one is impoverished by giving.

Happiness belongs to those who think of others.

All progress occurs because people dare to be different.

Risk

If you ride a tiger, you can't dismount.

Chinese saying

The higher up the ladder, the greater the fall.

The nearer the king, the nearer the gallows.

If you are too kind, you may attract the wrong kind of people.

There's a risk in crossing the street and there's a risk in not crossing the street.

Many things are sweetened by risk.

Ships fear fire more than water.

When skating on thin ice, speed is safety.

SADNESS

Sadness is not what we have but what we have missed.

It's sadness enough to have once been happy.

There is no greater sadness than remembering happy days past.

So much unnecessary sadness is caused by guilt!

All love ends in sadness – because death leaves one lover alone.

Nothing is sadder than the death of an illusion.

Sad is the person who has nothing but money.

How sad the words, "It might have been."

All passions have a touch of sadness.

They who are only wise lead a sad life.

To be loved and not know it – that's sad.

The tragedy is to have everything except the ability to enjoy it.

The greatest loss in life is not death – but what dies inside us while we live.

If we could not forget, we would never
be free from grief.

A great sorrow will drive out a lesser one.

Who weeps for others remembers himself.

Those whom the gods love die young.

The fairest silk is stained first.

Happiness is the interval between unhappiness.

Every time we say goodbye I die a little.

Song

A moment of time may make us unhappy for ever.

The greatest pains are those you can tell no-one.

We destroy ourselves by regret for yesterday and fear for tomorrow.

Forgetfulness helps ease our grief.

Loneliness robs us of our happiness and mocks our success.

We prefer strangers because they have not yet hurt us.

The greatest sorrows are those we cause ourselves.

From happiness to sorrow may take a moment – from sorrow to happiness may take years.

The saddest thing I can imagine is to get used to luxury.

Jesus wept.

Bible

How sad to see a beautiful theory
killed by a brutal fact.

Aldous Huxley

It's so sad to see beauty wasted.

How sad that bread is so dear and life is so cheap.

When I think of the good times
I've wasted having a good time!

Judy Garland

"We were all young and beautiful once," said Alice.

Misery is often the result of thinking too much.

Don't make two sorrows out of one.

If you expect nothing, you won't be disappointed.

Pain and boredom are the two main
causes of unhappiness.

The further you are from me, the closer I feel you.

Neapolitan song

SARCASM

If I dropped dead right now,
I'd be the happiest person alive.

Samuel Goldwyn

Those too busy doing good often find little time for
being good.

See a pin and pick it up and all day you'll have a pin.

The only use for higher mathematics is to be able to teach someone else higher mathematics.

Bertrand Russell

Opera is often better than it sounds.

He has the kind of face
– once seen is never remembered.

Oscar Wilde

"That's a nice dress you're wearing – was it your mother's?" said the Duke sarcastically.

SCOUNDRELS

Scoundrels are always sociable.

The bigger the rogue, the more convincing the lie.

Many kiss the baby for the sake of the nurse.

Sweet promises cost nothing.

If you want to be popular, pretend to be interested.

Always be sincere – even if you don't mean it.

Some people are too polite to be up to any good.

The ability to do nothing is the ability
to see others perish.

Selfishness often seems a quality that inspires love.

Secrets

The only real secrets are our sins.

Secrets are betrayed by the face.

The greatest pains are those you can tell no-one.

Tell secrets and you become their servant.

Your friend has a friend – so tell no secrets.

A person may be very secretive yet have no secrets.

When drink goes in, secrets come out.

Shallowness

Many people have character and nothing else.

Only the mediocre are always at their best.

Oscar Wilde

Many people go to church to air their finery.

None are so empty as those who are full of themselves.

Small minds are troubled by small things.

Those who know little often repeat it.

Shallow people believe in luck.

Seriousness is the refuge of the shallow.

Silence

Silence is the perfect expression of scorn.

Silence is the best substitute for intelligence.

Silence is a person's best argument.

A silent person tells us something.

More have regretted through speech
than through silence.

You have not converted someone just because you have silenced them.

No answer is a type of answer.

If silence is good for the wise,
how much better for the fool!

The cruellest lies are those told in silence.

A truth that remains silent becomes poisonous.

Silence may be equal to confession.

Sins

Sin is the root of sorrow.

A sin repeated seems permitted.

Every sin brings its own punishment.

We are imprisoned by our sins.

A sin in private is not a sin.

Cruelty is the greatest sin.

Those who steal to live do not necessarily sin.

St Aquinas

Little sins are great when great men commit them.

The lack of love is the greatest sin. ✓

It's not a sin to sell dear – but it is to give poor value.

We are not punished for our sins but by them.

"Can it be a sin if no harm is done?" asked Alice.

If it were not for fear, sinning would be enjoyable.

The sinner may be a better person than the one trying to convert him.

The only real secrets are our sins.

Fear is the best protection against sinning.

When we can sin no more, we repent.

If you enjoy it, it must be sinful.

Let he who is without sin cast the first stone. ✓

Jesus

Who looketh upon a woman in lust
commiteth adultery.

Jesus

Every sin can be absolved.

Your sins are forgiven because you loved much.

Jesus

Poverty is not the sin of the poor
but the sin of the rich.

Nudity is not in itself particularly erotic
– it's the intention of nudity that stimulates.

Smugness

Thanks to the beggar we may feel important.

In fair weather it's easy to be an atheist.

The satisfaction of success is to know only those who have not succeeded.

How satisfying to feel guilty when you have done nothing wrong.

The poor think God is on their side
– the rich know he is.

There is a lot of happiness in having what others cannot.

Solitude

Solitude gives us a glimpse of life's meaninglessness.

What fools call loneliness the wise call solitude.

Solitude is sometimes the best company.

The lone sheep is in danger from the wolf.

A contented life would be a life of busy solitude.

Who lives alone is either a saint or a devil.

Wishing to be on your own could be an inverted sense of superiority.

Safety lies in solitude.

Bread eaten in secret is pleasant.

Bible

You can be lonely on your own but even lonelier with the wrong person.

STUBBORNNESS

When the legend conflicts with the facts,
stick to the legend.

When you have made up your mind, don't confuse yourself with facts.

A long dispute often means both parties
are in the wrong.

We use reason to justify our prejudices.

We have boxes in our minds with labels on them.

The trouble is the fools are sure
and the learned have doubts.

Only strong characters can be influenced – the weak ones know it all.

Stupidity

Stupidity does not consist of having no ideas but of having stupid ones.

Every day stupid people say things
which are not stupid.

It's stupidity to live poor and die rich.

To be clever enough to get plenty of money you must be stupid enough to want it.

Courage is halfway between cowardice and stupidity.

A great deal of learning can be packed
into an empty head.

Don't be too clever for your own good.

Fools build houses – the wise live in them.

To pay in advance is to be served badly.

We mock what we don't understand.

To forgive easily is to invite insults.

Trusting a lot has ruined a lot.

Just pretending to be rich has kept many poor.

Look for the ridiculous in everything and you'll find it.

It is a mistake trying to be more agreeable
than you really are.

If it's not broken, don't try to mend it.

As a last resort, read the instructions.

To marry once is a duty; to marry twice is folly;
to marry three times is madness.

Oscar Wilde

Too much cleverness is folly.

Men are led by toys.

You always pay for your stupidity one way or another.

Stupidity is being unwilling to make use
of any knowledge.

One may appear sincere and still be stupid.

SUCCESS

Success has ruined many a person.

Success which costs too much must
be considered failure.

Success makes a fool seem wise.

Success has many friends.

Success often depends on negative rather
than positive qualities.

Success is one way of annoying your friends.

Success is being able to spend your life your own way.

Success is the best revenge.

Success may blind us to injustices.

The hard thing about success is having to keep it up!

There are successful men but no great ones.

The secret of success is to know only those who have not succeeded.

There is something about success which is displeasing.

If at first you don't succeed – that makes you average.

You must know failure before you know success.

Often the most unreasonable hopes have been the cause of great success.

If it were not for fools, the rest would not succeed.

The reward for success is success.

The tortoise wins the race while the hare is sleeping.

Too many people are ruined by too much.

Most things are easy if done willingly.

Some climb the ladder – others take the lift.

The first blow is half the battle.

To hit your target, aim a little above it.

To hit a bullseye, fire the arrow first, then draw the target round it.

To be able to succeed it's important that you appear successful.

To be successful, act big, think big and talk big.
Aristotle Onassis

Success is five per cent inspiration
and ninety-five per cent who you know.

Giving in may sometimes be the best way to succeed.

For us to be happy it's not only necessary that we must succeed but perhaps also that others must fail.

SUFFERING

To have never suffered is to have never been blessed.

The antidote for mental suffering is physical pain.

Through suffering we have consciousness.

Who loves much, suffers much.

Wisdom comes through suffering.

Through adversity we know ourselves.

Our misfortunes are sometimes a blessing in disguise.

Don't suffer in silence – it takes the pleasure out of it.

Suffering is real – pleasures are imagined.

Don't part from illusions – they keep us from suffering too much.

All who love suffer.

SURVIVING

Vanity is our survival kit – without it we would perish.

The only alternative to co-existence is co-destruction.

If you live among dogs, keep a stick.

Rudeness is the weak man's imitation of strength.

Fear preserves life.

Food, warmth and shelter are the essentials – the rest to some degree is luxury.

Humour protects us from stress.

When it thunders, the thief becomes honest.

When your neighbour's house is on fire, hurry to fetch water – for your own.

It is safer to be feared than loved.

Danger makes people devout.

One sword keeps another in its sheath.

Many a person's foul language has saved his sanity.

A drowning person is not troubled by rain.

Weak people need to be witty.

A coward may not be glorious but he will remain healthy.

When in trouble, the wicked repent.

We have to fight wars to abolish war.

Life would be impossible without a sense of humour.

Dreams are necessary for our survival.

It's a crazy world and only the maddest survive.

Healthy sharks eat wounded sharks.

Never panic – but if you do, make sure the first to panic is you.

Whatever doesn't kill us makes us stronger.

Nietzsche

TALK

Talk long enough and you will regret it.

Talk is cheap but it can't be bought back.

The tongue of the fool is his damnation.

Bible

A bore is a person who talks when you want him to listen.

Talk sense to a fool and he'll call you foolish.

Say nothing and they might think you a fool – say something and they will know you are.

Hasty speech has been the downfall of many.

If we say what we like, we may hear what we don't like.

A person may lack the power of conversation – but not the power of speech.

Fools are wise as long as they remain silent.

Be wise and hear – be a fool and speak.

We may regret our speaking but never our silence.

Beauty is best when silent.

Deeds are better than words.

Talk too much and you will soon say something you didn't intend to.

When nothing is known, we should be silent
– when everything is known, why speak?

The thoughtless are rarely wordless.

Watch out for the fellow who lets you do
all the talking.

The object of oratory is not truth but persuasion.

Machiavelli

The greatest talkers are often the least doers.

It's the second word that makes the quarrel.

In many words we lose the truth.

The fewer the words, the fewer the mistakes.

A spoken word cannot be recalled.

Look wise and say nothing – speech is only useful to conceal our thoughts.

Hear much – say little.

"Thank you" won't fill any purse.

A verbal contract is not worth the paper it's written on.

Samuel Goldwyn

Beware of words, for with words we lie.

W H Auden

Where there is no common language, there is suspicion.

We use the word "principle" when we cannot use reason.

We may forget blows but not words.

TEMPTATIONS

The best protection against temptation is cowardice.

Until you have been tempted, you don't know how honest you are.

An open door will tempt a saint.

If our parents had not been tempted, we would not be here.

Wealth is subject to more temptations than poverty.

It's not the bread but the butter and jam that makes the temptation.

The devil tempts us so he may punish us.

The temptations resisted in our youth are the ones we regret the most.

Virtue is not being tempted.

You never know what you might have done if you had been tempted.

Adam didn't want the apple for the apple's sake but because it was forbidden.

Don't worry about avoiding temptations – as we grow older they avoid us.

THIEVES

A thief believes everyone else also steals.

Many a person is saved from being a thief
by finding everything locked up.

Opportunity makes the thief.

It's not the mouse that's the thief
but the hole in the wall.

If you help a thief, you are as bad as a thief.

Minor thieves are hanged – major ones are honoured.

The receiver is as bad as the thief.

Beauty provokes a thief more than money.

Who marries a widow and three children
marries four thieves.

Give a thief a rope and he'll steal it.

If you don't steal, you won't feel guilty.

War makes thieves – peace hangs them.

A thief is sorry that he is caught – not that he is a thief.

THINKING

Thinking is not the same as knowing.

Nothing is ever said that has not been
thought out beforehand.

When all people think alike, no-one thinks very much.

Those who don't think much of themselves are better than they think.

There is nothing either good or bad, but thinking makes it so.

Shakespeare

To believe everything or to doubt everything is to stop thinking.

We think as we do mainly because others think so.

Misery is often the result of thinking too much.

He thinks too much: such men are dangerous.

Shakespeare

Some people never stop to think – others never think to stop.

We are the result of our thoughts.

We are what we think we are.

Think first – then speak.

Quoting from other people is a substitute for thinking for yourself.

You can't be happy if you think too much.

A conclusion is when you get tired of thinking.

Necessity is easier than thinking.

Often when we think we are thinking we are merely rearranging our prejudices.

We may not be responsible for our thoughts but we are for our deeds.

He who thinks he is wise is a fool.

A philosopher is one who doubts.

No bookmaker thinks gambling is a mug's game.

You're not happy unless you think you are.

Reason is the greatest enemy of faith.

Have an open face but conceal your thoughts.

To think evil is much the same as doing it.

Prejudices are a short cut to thinking.

A drunk person will say what a sober person is thinking.

You can educate a person but you can't make him think.

Learning is sometimes a convenient way of not having to think.

Once people begin to reason, all is lost.

Voltaire

If you think too much, you will probably find something to worry about.

Keep quiet and you will be thought a thinker.

TIME

Time doesn't go. Time stays – we go.

Time is the rider which breaks in youth.

I have wasted time – now time has wasted me.

Goethe

What may be done at any time may never be done.

Lazy people have no spare time.

There is a time to see and a time to look away.

The future often arrives before you are ready for it.

We are tomorrow's past.

The time to relax is when you don't have time to relax.

Nothing is worth more than this day.

Goethe

One today is worth two tomorrows.

Gather ye rosebuds while ye may.

Robert Herrick

A sack of gold won't buy a sack of time.

There never was a golden age.

An hour in the morning is worth two in the evening.

To live for the moment is not to deny the past.

"One of these days" is none of these days.

I have no time to be in a hurry.

Jerome K Jerome

O! Call back yesterday, bid time return.

Shakespeare

Love makes time pass and time makes love pass.

Heroes in war are an embarrassment in peace.

Today is the scholar of yesterday.

Better to arrive late than not at all.

Old age is always ten years ahead.

What's to come is unsure – come kiss me, sweet twenty – youth's stuff won't endure.

Shakespeare

It's not how long we live but how well we live.

The years go by so quickly – it's the days that are long.

A moment of time may make us happy forever.

"I am always punctually a half hour late," said the Duke in a superior voice.

The morning is wiser than the evening.

Russian saying

TROUBLES

Life is short but troubles make it long.

The troubles we bring on ourselves are often the hardest to bear.

A drowning person is not troubled by rain.

We all have the strength to endure the troubles of others.

If we all had our wishes, we would double our troubles.

When troubles end, so does life.

Other people's troubles are not wholly displeasing to us.

The world is full of troubles – but we can only feel our own.

A lot of troubles are man-maid.

Don't worry about tomorrow – who knows what today will bring!

To lend is to buy a quarrel.

Remembering our misfortunes gives us an additional misfortune.

A trouble shared is a trouble doubled.

Mark Twain

Bygone troubles are sweet to remember.

TRUTH

Truth looks different as we grow older.

Truth is its own witness.

Truth is lost in too much dispute.

Truth sits upon the lips of dying men.

Only the truth hurts.

Pilot asked, "What is truth?" Jesus didn't answer.

If we spoke the truth, life would be even more unbearable.

Repeat a thing often enough and it becomes the truth.

Sometimes kindness is better than truth.

Truth often depends on custom.

Give a man a mask and he will speak the truth.

Seldom is a splendid story wholly true.

Being sincere does not mean being truthful.

If you speak the truth, be prepared to be hurt.

A truth that remains silent becomes poisonous.

Some people can't tell the truth without lying.

All truth is relative – there is no absolute truth.

Descartes

In many words we lose the truth

There are always three sides to a story: yours, the other person's and the truth.

To conceal your motive, tell the truth.

Convictions are more dangerous enemies
of truth than lies.

In drink we mistake words for truth.

A half truth is a whole lie.

A big lie is often more plausible than the truth.

There is no greater lie than a truth misunderstood.

Cynicism is an unpleasant way of seeing the truth.

Those who don't change their opinions
love themselves more than they love truth.

A belief is not true just because it's convenient.

The devil sometimes speaks the truth.

History might be useful if it were true.

We don't always wish to hear the truth.

For the truth about yourself listen to your
best friend and your worst enemy.

The vices that really shock us are those
that are within us.

A mirror will tell you what your friends will not.

I don't mind lying but I hate inaccuracies.

Oscar Wilde

Perhaps we might prefer to be deceived.

If you tell the truth, you don't have to remember what
you said.

Better an ugly truth than a beautiful lie.

To be in the minority probably means
you're in the right.

When two sincere people argue over their beliefs, both
are right.

Why spoil a good story with facts?

The greater the truth, the greater the libel.

Truth turns into dogma as soon as it is disputed.

Don't insult people by telling them the truth.

TYRANNY

Tyranny leads by following the mob.

Tyranny is always better organised than liberty.

Tyranny feeds on fears.

When a tyrant dies, his rule is over – when a martyr
dies, his rule begins.

Every man has the seeds of tyranny within him.

Tyrants don't need any reason.

Remove the fear and you remove the power.

Henchmen can become worse than their masters.

If a person has no delicacy, he has you in his power.

There are no warlike people – only warlike leaders.

Man is born free but everywhere is in chains.

Rousseau

No-one is perfectly free until all are free.

A vain person can never really be ruthless.

Necessity is the argument of tyrants.

A tyrant doesn't mind being hated – as long as he is feared.

Revolution is the right of the slave.

You cannot shake hands with a clenched fist.

Gandhi

The greater the power, the greater the abuse.

The only thing necessary for the triumph of evil is for the good to do nothing.

No man can terrorise a whole nation unless we are all accomplices.

From fanaticism to barbarism is but a single step.

VALUES

Nothing is worth more than this day.

Goethe

Who overvalues himself will undervalue others.

To waste time is not to have discovered
the value of life.

The worth of a thing is what it will bring.

What costs nowt is worth nowt.

No-one is useless who lightens the burden of another.

What good is a gold cup if full of tears?

A pebble and a diamond feel the same
to a blind person.

All colours look alike in the dark.

Nothing is interesting if you are not interested.

Only the mediocre are always at their best.

Oscar Wilde

Good deeds remain good deeds, no matter
what the motive.

Men make houses – women make homes.

Before you borrow from a friend, decide which you
need most.

One today is worth two tomorrows.

While a cow can be milked it won't be slaughtered.

There is not a lot you can do with a prize once you have won it.

We often don't value what we already have.

All good things are cheap – all bad things are dear.

We must often accept second best as being best.

Every person is important to himself.

It's not a sin to sell dear – but it is to give poor value.

Rob me of the price but not of the quality.

The greatest pleasures are often the most pointless ones.

The price of umbrellas goes up when it rains.

One country's hero is another country's terrorist.

We are what we think we are.

An hour in the morning is worth two in the evening.

Those who don't think much of themselves may be better than they think.

Possessions are usually diminished by possessions.

When luxuries grow, so do necessities.

How many vices or virtues are really very important?

When an animal does it, we call it instinct – when we do it, we call it intelligence.

No human being is of great importance.

Plato

The certainties of one age are the problems of the next.

The quality is remembered long after the price is forgotten.

The saddest thing I can imagine is to
get used to luxury.

When you educate a man, you educate a person. When you educate a woman, you educate a family.

When is betrayal not betrayal? When it is business.

Rob me of the cost but not the quality.

The graveyards are full of indispensable men.

I have simple tastes – I only like the best.

Barbara Cartland

Life without industry is guilt.

Once you have tasted wine, who wants water?

Frank Sinatra

There are no wrong answers – only wrong questions.

An earthquake abroad may be a disaster but our toothache is an emergency.

VANITY

Vanity is the greatest of flatterers.

Vanity usually demands sacrifices.

Vanity made the revolution – liberty was only the pretext.

Napoleon

All is vanity – but we all need it.

Love is the vanity of two.

Doing good is also a form of vanity.

Vanity is our survival kit – without it we would perish.

One is vain by nature but honest by necessity.

Virtue brings honour – and honour brings vanity.

A vain person can never really be ruthless.

There is no love without vanity.

Vanity – all is vanity.

Bible

It is hard to dislike someone who praises you.

To refuse praise is to seek praise twice.

Every donkey loves to hear himself bray.

Pride often wears the cloak of humility.

To speak ill of someone is a dishonest way of praising ourselves.

We often need someone smaller than ourselves to make us feel bigger.

Every king needs a jester.

Many make themselves poor by trying not to appear poor.

When a proud man hears another praised he thinks himself injured.

What flatters a person is the thought that he is worth flattering.

Not talking about yourself is a form of hypocrisy.

Mediocre people often have the most acquired knowledge.

No-one is so lonely as he who loves only himself.

Shyness is often the result of having too high an opinion of yourself.

When we ask for an opinion we are merely seeking approval.

Nothing is easier than self-deception.

People are never more ridiculous than when they take themselves seriously.

A cockerel is very important on his own dunghill.

Wishing to be alone could be an inverted sense of superiority.

The most silent people are often those who think most highly of themselves.

God doesn't listen to the prayers of the proud.

We all love what we are good at.

To refuse praise is to desire to be praised even more.

All love is self-love.

VICE

Vice is its own punishment.

The vices that really shock us are those we are capable of ourselves.

When vices leave us – we flatter ourselves that we have left our vices.

Hate the sin and not the sinner.

Calculated virtue must be considered a vice.

Cruelty is the worst of all vices.

Evil is really a kind of religion – it implies intelligence and deliberate intent.

VICTORY

It's the last battle that counts.

You may lose everything but find yourself.

It's not how you start but how you finish.

To forgive is to gain a victory.

The robbed that smiles steals something from the thief.

Shakespeare

Tomorrow do your worst – for I have lived today.

John Dryden

What was hard to endure is sweet to recall.

One person with courage makes a majority.

Love conquers all. (*Amor vincit omnia.*)

The last enemy that is destroyed is death.

Bible

You may win the war but lose the peace.

The devil's greatest victory is to persuade us that he doesn't exist.

After the chase, the victory is often an anti-climax.

The harder the fight, the sweeter the victory.

No-one wins who doesn't fight.

Two dogs fight over a bone – the third one gets it.

History is written by the victors.

You can't hope to win unless you begin.

It's not the strongest who win but those who want it the most.

We hate to see a poor loser or a rich winner.

We may win at first but lose at last.

Virtue

Virtue is praised but disliked.

Virtue is not being tempted.

When we enjoy giving, then giving is no longer a virtue.

It is easy to be virtuous when we have no other choice.

Virtue is its own reward.

Virtue is so praiseworthy we often practise it out of self-interest.

Some people with great virtues are disagreeable – while some with great vices are quite agreeable.

Unnatural are those who prefer virtue to bodily pleasure.

Virtue brings honour – and honour brings vanity.

Calculated virtue must be considered a vice.

Force and fraud are virtues in war.

Patience is despair disguised as virtue.

We are often liked more for our faults than for our virtues.

Virtue is often a matter of necessity.

Tolerance is the virtue of the person with no convictions.

VISION

Vision is the art of seeing the invisible.

Pope Pius X

When it's dark enough you can see the stars.

The wise see enough and no more.

The heart sees better than the eyes.

I shut my eyes in order to see.

St Augustine

The closer you are, the less you can see.

Some things have to be believed to be seen.

Being unable to see what you don't want to see is a great advantage.

War

War is a coward's way of escaping the
problems of peace.

War is a man's life and women and children's death.

War takes man's highest quality to do man's
lowest deeds.

War makes good history but peace makes poor reading.

War begins in the minds of men.

War makes thieves and peace hangs them.

In wars over men's beliefs, women and children
get killed.

All wars are civil wars because we are all brothers.

Heroes in war are an embarrassment in peace.

In peace, sons bury their mothers. In war, mothers bury
their sons.

Even the winners lose in war.

For war, one side is enough; for peace, you need two.

Old men make wars – young men die in them.

Force and fraud are virtues in war.

As long as war is looked upon as wicked it will have its fascination.

In modern war now, soldiers no longer kill soldiers but machines kill communities.

A nation is only at peace with itself when it is at war.

In the long run all wars are lost.

A uniform provides half a man's valour.

Soldiers win battles – generals get the credit.

If one soldier knew what the other was thinking, there would be no war.

Children play at being soldiers – and soldiers play at being children.

One sword keeps another in its sheath.

Vanity made the revolution – liberty was only the pretext.

Napoleon

War is the continuation of politics.

Guns don't kill people – people kill people.

We make war so we may live in peace.

It's dreadful to think our morality is controlled by geography.

Men are led by toys.

Peace is that time between wars.

Sports are an imitation of fighting.

It's old men and politicians who start wars.

History proves war is better at abolishing nations than nations at abolishing war.

The only alternative to co-existence is co-destruction.

The atom bomb has changed everything except our thinking – thus we are drifting towards catastrophe.

Albert Einstein

In Flanders fields the poppies blow
Between the crosses row on row.

John McCrae

Better to have a just war than an unjust peace.

To kill a person may be the least injury you can do to him.

When we say 'to die for our country', we really mean 'to kill for our country'.

Praiseworthy deeds in war are punishable crimes in peace.

If you want peace, be ready for war.

We have to fight wars to abolish war.

You may win the war but lose the peace.

When the rich wage war, it's the poor who die.

Take the uniform away from the generals and how many wars would be started?

Nowadays it may be safer to be a soldier on the battlefield than a civilian in the market place.

Make love not war – but both can kill you.

Pacifism is simply a disguise for cowardice.

Adolf Hitler

WARNING

Everybody's friend is nobody's friend.

Few can do us good – but many can do us harm.

If you lie with dogs, you will rise with fleas.

Don't push a lapdog too far – he may turn into a Rottweiler.

Honey catches more flies than vinegar.

There are no small enemies.

Let other shipwrecks be our warning.

If you dig a pit, you might fall into it.

Bible

Where the carcass is – that's where the vultures are gathered.

Bible

The way to be safe is never to feel secure.

We become like those we associate with.

Even a bargain costs money.

The light at the end of the tunnel may be an oncoming train.

Those over-friendly may be cheating you.

Greed and desperation know no limit.

Run after two hares and you catch none.

If you live among dogs, keep a stick.

There are two tragedies: one is not getting what you wish for – the other is getting what you wish for.

Let he who seeks revenge dig two graves.

Chinese saying

Good bargains empty purses.

Whoever does you a bad turn won't forgive you.

He who walks in the jungle will one day meet a tiger.

Yin Yin Fu

WEAKNESS

All cruelty springs from weakness.

The weak who know how to play on their weakness become strong.

Weak people, when united, become strong.

Sweetness is often a disguise for weakness.

Quarrels are the weapons of the weak.

The weak are often the first to turn to violence.

Power corrupts a few but weakness corrupts many.

Rudeness is the weak man's imitation of strength.

A person's weakness is often the most likeable thing about him.

Act like a lamb and the wolves will get you.

Weak people need to be witty.

Tolerance is often a form of cowardice.

It doesn't worry the fox the number of sheep there are.

A man may resist a sound argument
yet fall at a single glance.

Given the choice, we usually follow the herd.

The greater the man, the greater the weakness.

Lloyd George

Try to be reasonable and it will be taken for weakness.

WEALTH

Wealth infatuates as well as beauty.

Wealth is not what you have but what you enjoy.

Wealth is subject to more temptations than poverty.

Wealth makes many friends.

To be content with little is a great wealth.

A person's wealth is his enemy.

An obsession to increase wealth
is a main source of misery.

Misers are kind people – they leave
their wealth for others.

Wisdom without wealth is not worth a lot.

Riches increase rather than satisfy desires.

An ounce of fortune is worth more than a sack of gold.

Sad is the person with nothing but money.

If you have one watch you know what time it is
– if you have two you are never sure.

Golden shackles are worse than iron ones.

Gandhi

Wealth is not a lot of pleasure by itself
– it must be shown off to be enjoyed.

Behind every great fortune is a great crime.

You are rich if you have no debts.

A rich person is not short of friends.

The man who dies rich dies in disgrace.

Andrew Carnegie

The rich man's joke is always funny.

To become rich is not the end of our worries
but the change of our worries.

You can't be too thin or too rich.

Duchess of Windsor

Rich people are only poor people with more.

WISDOM

Wisdom may increase with age but so does folly.

Wisdom is being wise at the right time.

Wisdom without wealth is not worth a lot.

Wisdom comes through suffering.

To recognise folly is the first step of wisdom.

We are all a little foolish but wisdom consists of not exceeding the limit.

We can give advice but not the wisdom to go with it.

A teetotaller rarely possesses wisdom.

Without experience there is little wisdom.

The first sign of love is the last sign of wisdom.

No person is ever as wise as he appears to be.

The wisest prophets make sure of the event beforehand.

The young are still wise enough to make fools of themselves.

If we had our chance again, would we all be wiser?

No person becomes wise just from learning.

To live without a little foolishness
is not as wise as you think.

It's hard to love and be wise.

A white beard doesn't make a person wise.

Too much cleverness is folly.

You get wise from listening and regret from speaking.

He who knows he's a fool is not a great fool.

Better to weep with the wise than
laugh with the fool.

You can pass on knowledge but not wisdom.

When nothing is known, we should be silent
– when everything is known, why speak?

The wise can play the fool
– but a fool can't play the wise.

The wise may change their mind
– but the fool never will.

The wise will learn from everyone.

The wise will see enough and no more.

The wise will do at once what the fool
will do eventually.

The wise will get more from their enemies than the
fool will get from their friends.

The wise know what to overlook.

The wise man wants for nothing.

A wise person knows things – a shrewd person knows people.

A wise person does not need a weapon.

A person is wise when he doesn't appear too clever.

Give instructions to the wise and they will be yet wiser.

The fool may ask questions that the wise cannot answer.

In the company of fools, a wise man looks foolish.

You are wise if few things annoy you.

The most learned people are not always the most wise.

He who thinks he is wise is a fool.

No person is born wise.

A word to the wise is enough.

We are all wise in our own eyes.

They who are only wise lead a sad life.

Better to play the fool a little than to be thought a complete fool.

Fools build houses – wise men live in them.

Even the fool – when he holds his tongue –
is considered wise.

Wishes

Be careful what you wish for – you might get it.

The way to punish someone is to
grant them all their wishes.

If we had all our wishes, we would double our troubles.

There are two tragedies: one is not getting what you wish for, the other is getting what you wish for.

We would often be sorry if our wishes were granted.

Wishing may be better than having.

A man is led the way he wishes to follow.

Wives

When someone steals your wife, the best revenge is let him keep her.

Never make a pretty woman your wife.

Jamaican saying

Old maids make devoted wives.

Ascend a step to choose a friend – descend a step to choose a wife.

Chinese saying

An obedient wife rules her husband.

I have a beautiful wife – everybody loves her.

It's a sad house where the hen crows
louder than the cockerel.

The most fascinating women seldom
make the best wives.

Better to have a plain wife for yourself than a beautiful wife for others.

An old maid, when she marries,
becomes a young bride.

WOMEN

Women inspire men to greatness – then prevent them from achieving it.

Women cannot forgive failure.

A woman's tears are a form of bribery.

Women don't realise the power of their flirtations.

A woman's weakness is her strength.

A woman's beauty may be fatal to her.

Woman was God's second blunder.

A woman will not forgive a man for the sacrifices
he makes on her account.

A woman will start a row then ask you to apologise.

There are no unseduceable women – only inept men.

It takes a clever woman to handle a foolish man.

In her first passion a woman loves her lover,
In all the others all she loves is love.

It's better for a woman to be looked
over than to be overlooked.

Mae West

The only chaste woman is one that has never been chased.

Those who complain about women usually have a particular woman in mind.

Once made equal to men
– women become their superiors.

Socrates

It's hard to be a pretty woman without
causing a little trouble.

There is no heavier load than a light woman.

Men who cherish the highest respect for women
are seldom popular with them.

In the dark, all women are fair.

Nothing spoils a romance so much as a sense of humour in a woman.

Men make houses – women make homes.

There is a harlot in every woman – that is their attraction.

Oscar Wilde

A rich widow cries with one eye and laughs with the other.

It was a man's world until the arrival of Eve.

If it wasn't for women, money would have little meaning.

Aristotle Onassis

I married beneath me – all women do.

Nancy Astor

When you educate a man, you educate a person – when you educate a woman you educate a family.

Wrinkles on a man are considered experience – on a woman, age.

Ageing is when a woman looks in the mirror and suddenly sees her mother.

All women are the same height lying down.

Only women should get married.

Oscar Wilde

WORK

Work is less boring than amusing yourself.

Work is a refuge for people with nothing better to do.

Oscar Wilde

Work is the best remedy for grief.

If you enjoy work, it's not work.

No rest is worth having, unless it follows work.

The hardest work is doing nothing.

Oh, what harm is done in the belief that work is honourable!

It's not work but worry that kills.

Happiness makes us lazy
– the miserable seem to work better.

One lawyer makes work for another.

The object of work is to gain leisure.

In all labour there is profit.

Bible

No labour dishonours a person.

Busy people find more leisure time.

Start many things and you will finish few.

Idleness is a vocation.

Jerome K Jerome

Nothing difficult is easy.

Work like a navvy and you'll stay a navvy.

It is boredom, not hard work, that kills.

You can get rich from work
– often from someone else's.

All work and no play makes Jack a dull boy – and Jill a wealthy widow.

The harder you work, the luckier you get.

WORRY

Worry won't pay your debts.

An empty purse fills the face with wrinkles.

Hurrying is a visible form of worrying.

It's not work but worry that kills.

With riches come worries.

It's often the little things that break us up.

Many a person's foul language has saved his sanity.

Laughter reduces blood pressure.

A boiling kettle will overflow.

Can you remember your worries of a year ago?

It's the last drop that makes the overflow.

The worst punishment is a sleepless night.

Humour protects us from stress.

The time to relax is when you don't have time to.

If you think too much, you will probably find something to worry about.

Worry is fear without a decision.

To become rich is not the end of our worries but the change of our worries.

YOUTH

Youth lasts longer than we think – it's old age that's unexpected.

Youth is the one thing that never returns.

Youth is a very temporary state of affairs.

If youth is a fault, then it's soon cured.

Time is the rider which breaks in youth.

An idle youth makes a needy old age.

The indiscretions of our youth are the happy memories of our old age.

Common sense consists of the prejudices laid down in our youth.

The young are still wise enough to make fools of themselves.

The only difference between the toys of the young and the toys of the old is the price.

The very young and the very old are usually the most selfish.

The young think the world was made for them.

"If society does not care for us, why should we care for society?" said the lad.

My salad days – when I was green in judgment.

Shakespeare

Old men make wars – young men die in them.

When all the world is young, lad . . .
And every lass a queen.

Charles Kingsley

The ability to see beauty is the ability to stay young.

Better to waste your youth than to do nothing with it.

To get back to your youth just repeat your follies.

Have ideals in your youth – because you won't in old age.

In youth the body grows faster than the brain.

What's to come is unsure – come kiss me, sweet twenty – youth's stuff won't endure.

Shakespeare

In growing up we cross the line from innocence to corruption.

When I was young – before I knew I was happy.

Dylan Thomas